DEFINED

Who God Says You Are

PRISCILLA SHIRER

LifeWay Press® | Nashville, Tennessee

EDITORIAL TEAM

Student Ministry Publishing

BEN TRUEBLOOD
Director, Student Ministry

JOHN PAUL BASHAM
Manager, Student
Ministry Publishing

KAREN DANIEL
Editorial Team Leader

MORGAN HAWK
Content Editor

AMANDA MEJIAS
Content Specialist

SARAH SPERRY
Graphic Designer

Requests for permission should be addressed in
writing to LifeWay Press;
One LifeWay Plaza;
Nashville, TN 37234.

ISBN: 978-1-5359-6006-9
Item Number: 005815892
Dewey decimal classification: 248.83
Subject headings: RELIGION/
Christian Ministry/Youth

To order additional copies of this resource, write
to LifeWay Church Resources Customer Service;
One LifeWay Plaza; Nashville, TN 37234-0113; fax
615.251.5933; phone toll free 800.458.2772; email
orderentry@lifeway.com; order online at
www.lifeway.com.

Printed in the United States of America.

Author photo by Meshali Mitchell.

Student Ministry Publishing
LifeWay Christian Resources
One LifeWay Plaza
Nashville, TN 37234

CONTENTS

PRISCILLA SHIRER

Priscilla Shirer is a homemade cinnamon roll baker, Bible teacher, actress, and best-selling author who didn't know she was on *The New York Times* Best Sellers List (*Fervent*) until somebody else told her. Because who has time to check lists when you are busy cleaning up after (and trying to satisfy the appetites of) three rapidly growing sons?

Priscilla is passionate about sharing God's Word with women of all ages, both the young and the young at heart. Put a Bible in her hand and a message in her heart, and you'll see why thousands meet God in powerful, personal ways through her words. She and her husband, Jerry, founded Going Beyond Ministries and count it as their privilege to serve believers across the entire spectrum of the body of Christ.

For the past twenty years, Priscilla has been in full-time ministry to women, speaking internationally and authoring more than two dozen books and Bible studies on a myriad of different biblical topics and personalities including *Discerning the Voice of God, Gideon, Jonah*, and *The Armor of God*. Now she is excited to share this most recent Bible study, *Defined*, with you.

HOW TO USE

In this book, you will find eight weeks of group sessions, seven weeks of personal study, and a leader guide. Each session consists of a group guide followed by five days of personal study. As you begin your group time, watch the video to hear from the heart of the author. There is also a leader guide included in the back of this study with some helpful tips to use during group time. As you close group time, encourage students to complete the personal days that follow the group sessions. Once girls have completed this study, they will better understand who God is and what it means to be created in His image. Then we can know exactly who we are and that we were created just the way God planned and for exactly this time.

BIBLE STUDY BOOK

Listed below are the different elements in the Bible study book.

Group Discussion
Questions and personal connections are provided to help guide the conversation.

Personal Study
Five days of personal Bible study will help reinforce the theme and provide an opportunity to study passages not covered in the group discussion.

Leader Guide
The leader guide at the back of the study provides ideas for activities and deeper group discussions.

SESSION OUTLINE

Design your group sessions to fit the space, time, and needs of your girls. The following is a sample group session outline that you can adapt.

1. Press Play
Review the material in the previous week's personal Bible study and watch the video.

2. Let's Talk
Scripture and discussion questions are provided to help foster conversation among the group.

3. Closing
Answer some final questions together and spend some time looking at the upcoming personal study days. Close the session with prayer.

A NOTE FROM PRISCILLA

AT CHRISTMAS one year, my siblings and I got a Big Wheel—a brightly colored, low-slung take on a tricycle that was a kid's dream. Each of us, all under ten years of age, were thrilled. The dawn of electric scooters and hoverboards hadn't yet crested the modern-day horizon, and this mobile toy was everything.

But it took a while to get to the fun part where we could start riding it up and down the driveway of our childhood home, because the Big Wheel underneath the Christmas tree on that bright morning was not ready to ride. It was an enormous box with pieces of an unassembled Big Wheel inside, which we begged our dad to hurry up and open and get busy putting together. And he did—or at least he tried—a task we four kids didn't make any easier on him by pelting him every few minutes with our impatience. He grew frustrated and tired as he worked to fit the oddly shaped pieces together and make the large wheel up front respond to pedal strokes.

Finally, after realizing more than an hour had gone by, our mom voiced the one thing that helped get things moving in the right direction. She strode into the garage where my poor Daddy was still feverishly trying to make connections between all these various parts of the Big Wheel strewn across the floor, and said, "Honey, why don't you read the instructions?"

Makes sense. The manufacturer is the one who knows how things are supposed to fit together. The manufacturer is able to accurately identify all the pieces and put them into place, into a completed whole. And to top it off, the manufacturer even provides a manual to read so we can know how to handle his creation the way he intended.

I think you know what I'm getting at. The God who made you has given you His Word so that not only can you understand all the pieces of your identity that make you unique and special, but you can put those pieces together successfully and get out there and ride. Take this show on the road. Actually live the life He's imagined and made possible for you. He's given you the instructions that show you how.

And, hey, we all need them—black girls, brown girls, white girls, and every color of girl in between. Tall girls, short girls, athletic girls, academic girls, poor girls, even rich girls. Straight-haired blond girls, curly-headed brunette girls. Suburban girls and inner-city girls. All of us girls—all of us women—need good instructions.

Because, listen to me, if you don't see the value in consulting the instruction manual, you'll end up with some disjointed and ill-fitting parts—things you'll still be trying to undo and refit in the later decades of your life. That's because a lot of the advice and direction you'll receive from the culture and social media and your peers—even from yourself—will be flat-out inaccurate.

- Ever-changing standards of beauty will whisper that you're *ugly*.
- A teacher who embarrasses you or a camp counselor who overlooks you will make you feel *worthless*.
- The clique that won't accept you or people who refuse to include you will communicate you're *unwanted*.
- People who laughed at you instead of affirming and celebrating you will make you feel *unloved*.
- That guy who won't look at you or who brushed you aside instead of treasuring you will communicate that you are *rejected*.
- The social media feeds that haunt you, displaying the lives of more popular, seemingly more perfect people than yourself, make you feel *invisible*.
- The tears you cry, the hurts you nurse, the wounds you bear deep inside your heart will scream that you're *broken*.
- The secret habit you indulge, again and again, hopeless that you can ever change, will continually leave you feeling *bound*.
- The coach that keeps nit-picking you, convincing you that you'll never measure up, will make you feel *inadequate*.
- That horrible mistake you made or that terrible sin you committed will sneer at you, shame you, and say you're *unforgivable*.
- The lust that you willingly gave into, or the innocence that evil stole from you, will keep whispering that you are *impure*.
- The circumstances surrounding your birth or, worse, the people who bring it up again to hurt you at your most vulnerable moments, tell you that you're a *mistake*.

These labels play on a never-ending loop in your mind, like lyrics from a song.

- "I'm a mistake."
- "I'm dirty."
- "I'm horrible."
- "I'm stupid."
- "I'm worthless."
- "I'm unloved."
- "I'm forgotten."
- "I'm unforgivable."
- "I'm unacceptable."

If you're not careful, little sister, this narrative will define your life. You'll start living down to the names that your circumstances have given you, instead of living up to the authentic narrative that God has made rightfully yours.

I want so desperately to tell you—just because you feel something, or have done something, or have been told something, or have experienced something doesn't mean you *are* something. You are only who the manufacturer says you are. He is the only One with the authority to give you your name. And because He passionately desires for you to understand this, He has spelled it out in black and white for you to read and know and believe and implement into your daily life.

Will you give me eight weeks to prove it to you? Eight weeks that could change the next eight decades of your life.

I am who God says I am.

I can do what God says I can do.

I can become exactly what

God says I can become.

I'm not defined by my feelings,

my weaknesses, or my inclinations,

and I will not devalue what He has

made me to be by comparing it

to what seems better and

brighter in someone else.

I am coming out of the lies.

I am coming into the light.

I will praise you because I have been
remarkably and wondrously made. Your works
are wondrous, and I know this very well.

PSALM 139:14

Week One

❧⟶ ⟜ ⟜ ⟜ ❧

UNIQUELY CREATED

PRESS PLAY

Use the space below to follow along and take any notes as you watch the video for Week 1.

What have you struggled to accept about yourself?

Only the _____ can define His _____ .

I will give thanks to You, for I am _____ and _____ made (Ps. 139:14, NASB).

Uniqueness and being _____ is not a liability.

How does gratitude grant you the freedom to be you?

You are who your _____ says you are.

How can you be thankful for who God has made you to be? How can you celebrate and affirm others in their differences?

AS A WIFE, mom, daughter, aunt, writer, speaker, and resident laundry woman/ homework checker/dinner fixer/bathroom cleaner–trust me, there's a lot of TV I miss. But thanks to Hulu, I was able to catch up on one particular series recently. It was already on season six in real time, which meant if I started with season one, episode one, I had *tons* of new drama and story lines to watch. Hour after hour. Back to back. To back? (Should I watch another?) To back? (Maybe just one more? Maybe?) To back.

You know what I'm talking about. Grab the chips and push the play button.

The other night as I was watching a particular episode play out, it made me think of you and about this study we're starting. In one memorable scene, a woman was sitting in a counselor's office trying to get her life straightened out–which can be quite a difficult thing to do, not only in TV shows but in real life, too. The wise therapist asked her a simple, straightforward question to get the conversation going: "Are you a good mother?"[1]

What?! You could see the indignation run right down her spine. "I'm a great mother!" she answered, quickly and confidently, not hesitating for a split-second before going into all of her reasons.

The therapist raised his hand to slow her down. He asked her to close her eyes and count to ten before answering the next question. Then he calmly, methodically, asked her the exact same question again, punctuating each word this time with a dramatic pause: "Are. You. A. Good. Mother?"

This time she paused, swallowing her bravado, thinking deeply. The moment's delay allowed opportunity for her fears, anxieties, failures, and weaknesses to bubble up to the surface of her previously calloused heart. Tears began falling from her eyes as honesty did its work. You could see the question sinking in. You heard the truth finally coming out.

Time and deep thought can really bring us to a place of authenticity and vulnerability. So I've got a really simple, straightforward question for you, too:

Who are you?

Answer this question quickly and without really thinking. Just write down the first thoughts that come to your mind. (Single words and phrases. Adjectives, both negative and positive, that quickly describe you.)

When I asked this same question on Twitter, I heard things like …

Strong · Stressed · Independent · Caring · Fat
Insecure · Failure · Smart · Crazy · Depressed
Fierce · Hopeless · Introverted · Gentle · Outgoing
Hardworking · Emotional · Nerdy · Moody · Blessed
Creative · Struggling · Driven · Loving

When you've finished crafting your first response, consider this: Was it easier for you to come up with negative characteristics or positive ones? Why do you think that is?

Now, I'm going to ask you again. And this time, I want you to close your eyes, take a deep breath, and let a few moments pass while you listen to God, while you listen to your soul, while you think back on what your life has been like–the good and bad, the highs and lows, the flaws and labels, the doubts and beliefs. Ask the Lord to bring to mind some of the stuff He wants you to deal with throughout this study. Let it just bubble up naturally. And as He places words and insights and answers into your head, write down as many of them as you feel comfortable listing in your book today. (You may want to come back later and add a few more. I actually want you thinking about this question a lot. Not just now, but frequently.)

Who (dramatic pause). Are (dramatic pause). You?

Let's hear it.

Give me more.

Is that all? You sure?

It really is amazing the deeper levels you can discern by absorbing a question and pondering it a second time. Watch Jesus do this same sort of thing with His disciples in Matthew 16:13-17.

Compare Jesus' question in verse 13 with His question in verse 15. What's the difference?

Now compare their answers in verse 14 with Peter's answer in verse 16. Their first answers came largely from public opinion. Where did Jesus say Peter's answer came from? (See verse 17.)

Why do you think God might wait to reveal something to you until He has more of your attention, until you've truly invested yourself in wanting to know?

Look back at the second set of attributes you wrote down, as well as the ones you wrote at first. Where do you believe these answers of yours mostly stem from? I'll give you some choices. Check any that apply.

☐ **How you've always thought of yourself**

☐ **What other people think or say about you (family, coach, friend, etc.)**

☐ **Things that have happened to you in the past (both good and bad)**

☐ **Influences from culture (TV, social media, movies, magazines)**

☐ **Your own past behaviors and attitudes**

☐ **Christian beliefs and teaching**

☐ **Somewhere else:** _____

This study is all about your *identity*. Who you really are. And let me tell you, right up front here—as I said to you in the intro to this whole study—the way you *feel* is not necessarily who you *are*.

So as you look back at the things you just wrote, some of them most likely do contain elements of your true identity, yet some of them probably reflect a few distortions based on the devil's lies and his ability to convince you that you're somebody based on your past, your behaviors, or illegitimate labels placed on you by others. This struggle between a woman's God-given identity and the one she often comes to believe about herself is continuous and ongoing. So, right here at your young age, it's time to call a thing a thing and expose the strategies of the enemy to deceive you, because they're designed to steer you away from your genuine identity. And we're just not having any of that.

So as we wrap up for today, I want you to continue to consider the things you've started thinking about, and also contemplate this online definition of *identity*:

"the fact of being who or what a person or thing is."[2]

Throughout the next eight weeks, this is what you and I are going to pursue: actually being and becoming who we really are and who we were really created to be. We'll be overcoming the lies we're constantly being fed and the distortions we're struggling to stand against. We'll think through some vital aspects of identity and answer questions like …

- Why is a strong sense of your true identity important?

- What kinds of false perspectives do you carry that impact your behavior?

- Who has the authority to determine your identity?

- How can God help you redefine yourself by what He says about you?

- How can you adapt your behavior to align with what you know about the identity He's given you?

- How can you express your individuality through the lens of your God-given identity?

Because here's the thing: You'll spend your whole life either (1) trying to be and become something you were never meant to be, or (2) discovering who you've been all along and investing yourself in that sure direction. The first path is exhausting, frustrating, soul-killing. (Have you noticed?) The second path is lined with enjoyment, freedom, and fulfillment with the real, honest-to-goodness ability to be uniquely you and to reach your divinely ordained potential without being hampered by perfectionism, fear, and crippling insecurity.

Take a moment to write a definition of identity in your own words.

How is a description of someone different from their identity?

I am so honored to sit across from you here as your teacher and sister in Christ. I'm no expert, just a girl who's lived a little longer than you, made some mistakes, dusted herself off, received grace, and started over again. So we'll grow together and explore this "Who Are You?" question from lots of different biblical angles, gaining clarity on so many of the profoundly important issues that arise from it and how it impacts your relationships, choices, and behaviors. And as we do, along the way–both in these group sessions as well as privately throughout the week–I truly believe the answers we find will change the course of your entire life.

DESTINATIONS

> I will praise you because I have been
> remarkably and wondrously made.
> **PSALM 139:14**

I HAVE a gorgeous niece named Kariss. She is a super-creative, ultra-entrepreneurial young woman who runs her own photography business and creates the most incredible images for her blogs and social media feeds. She's also a computer geek who has her finger on the pulse of advancements in technology.

Kariss made an interesting observation lately. She said she can always tell if a person was born pre-2000 or afterward by whether or not they give specific driving directions. She giggles every time she hears older people try to tell each other how to get somewhere by drawing a map or by detailing step-by-step, turn-by-turn instructions. Do you ever hear your parents or grandparents or other adults do that? Probably.

For it was you who created my inward parts; you knit me together in my mother's womb. I will praise you because I have been remarkably and wondrously made. Your works are wondrous, and I know this very well. My bones were not hidden from you when I was made in secret, when I was formed in the depths of the earth.
PSALM 139:13-15

But you never do that, do you? Because if you're supposed to meet a friend or find a place you've never been before, all you need is the address. Punch it into your phone, and your favorite navigational app will tell you exactly how to get there.

Well, you and I are on a journey here. We want to reach a specific location. We want to get to the place where we truly understand our identity and are living free of others' expectations and pressures. In order to get there, however, we need to put in some reliable addresses—locations we know are the right ones. Because as long as we plug in the right address, we can be sure it's going to take us to the right place.

I've placed in the margin a good address for us to start our journey. Read it slowly and prayerfully. Consider also looking it up in several different Bible translations.

Either in your Bible or in the margin, underline the words that stand out most clearly to you. Then tell me here why they caught your attention.

One of the most exciting ways to study the Bible and really understand what God wants us to see is to learn what the words meant in their original languages, and then find other Scripture addresses where those words also appear.[3] Being able to analyze how God used an identical word elsewhere, in another context, is a strategy I use all the time in my Bible study to give me a more comprehensive feel for what He means.

Let's take, for example, the word "wondrously," also translated "wonderfully." The Hebrew word that's translated "wondrously" in Psalm 139:14 actually shows up many times in the Old Testament. I'd like to draw your attention to two in particular. In each of them, God is speaking to Moses—first, as He was delivering the children of Israel from Egypt; second, as He was leading them toward the promised land.

Read Exodus 3:20 and Exodus 34:10 in the margin. Circle the one word in each verse that sounds the most like something "wondrous" or "wonderful."

Now think critically about the verses you just read:

1. Who is accomplishing the words you circled?

2. What makes these tasks unique from anything a human could do?

3. What was meant to be the outcome of God's "miracles" in Exodus 3:20?

4. What was meant to be the outcome of His "wonders" in Exodus 34:10?

If you were explaining to someone what any of these words imply and what they accomplished, what would you say?

In each of these verses, the Creator planned and performed specific, extraordinary, miraculous acts that were so eye-opening and jaw-dropping that no human could duplicate them, and no one who encountered them could remain unaffected. Whether friend or foe, whether ally or enemy, everyone who saw the "miracles" and "wonders" of God on display was moved in their hearts and became clearly aware of His purposes.

When I stretch out my hand and strike Egypt with all my miracles that I will perform in it, after that, he will let you go.
EXODUS 3:20

And the LORD responded: "Look, I am making a covenant. I will perform wonders in the presence of all your people that have never been done in the whole earth or in any nation. All the people you live among will see the LORD's work, for what I am doing with you is awe-inspiring."
EXODUS 34:10

And the same wonderful word that describes what God did in the Book of Exodus and the effect it had on the people who witnessed it is the same word in Psalm 139 that describes how "wondrously" He made you!

What does the "wondrous" way you were created tell you in terms of:

The same "wondrous" word from Psalm 139:14 is translated in a verse in Exodus as "distinguished." Look up Exodus 33:16. (Your version might say "distinct" or "separated" or "special" or "set apart.") How does this word add even more depth to your understanding of who you were made to be?

1. The fact that you are unique and cannot be replicated.

_____

_____

_____

_____

_____

2. The effect of your life and testimony on other people.

_____

_____

_____

_____

_____

You, girl, are a miracle. Your racial background, body shape, unique facial features, and hair texture are all an expression of the image of God. And even if you never hear others say it, the people who meet you—when you're being who God created you to be, not trying to be somebody you're not—are interacting with a literal, living, breathing miracle. And like all of God's miracles, your life will leave a lasting impact on them if you'll simply be yourself, surrendered to God, molded by His Spirit, and on mission for Him.

What are some of your most distinctive physical features and personality characteristics? Which of these characteristics are celebrated in your culture, and which are devalued?

What aspect of your physical body do you most struggle to enjoy?

What aspects of your personality feel more like liabilities than assets?

Explain the circumstances that have led you to feel and think this way about yourself.

My friend Kris was eighteen years old when a would-be boyfriend convinced her that she was too fat to be his date to the prom. As a result, she spent her senior year too consumed with obsessive exercise and not eating to make any enjoyable memories at all. It made her feel exhausted, frail, and on edge. Then a month before prom, despite her investment in her physical appearance, the guy asked someone else to the dance anyway. She wishes now—as a young, newly married woman in her twenties—that she could go back and tell her eighteen-year-old self the truth of Psalm 139 instead of ruining her last year of high school on the opinion of a pimply-faced boy.

Listen, whenever someone—a boy, a coach, teachers, or even a well-meaning loved one— makes you feel like you're anything less than a miracle, take back the reins and tell yourself the truth of Psalm 139, literally and out loud:

I am a miracle!

You are a demonstration of the creative genius of Almighty God, and the world is waiting to encounter the miracle of who He created you to be.

End today's lesson by writing out a short prayer of thanksgiving to God. Even if you don't feel special or you've been told you're less than miraculous, declare the truth in your prayer. Thank Him for the miracle He's created you to be.

HE SEES, HE KNOWS

LORD, you have searched me and known me.
PSALM 139:1

NO ONE KNOWS you like your Creator does. Every single quirk, uniqueness, weakness, or deficiency that your friends and family know about (and perhaps sometimes have a difficult time understanding or tolerating) is already known by God. But here's the best part: no matter what flaws you have or mistakes you may have made, He loves you just the same and intends to use every part of you as an instrument for His glory to be displayed. Every single part. Even the hard-to-accept parts. You have been intentionally designed, and you are crafted in His image.

Today, let's mine more treasures like these from Psalm 139.

I've printed a long passage in the margin of your book. These are the first six verses from Psalm 139. And, again, I want you to underline some specific words and phrases.

Look for any words or short statements that identify an action God takes concerning you. You should be able to find almost ten of them, depending on how narrowly you isolate things.

Craft a long run-on sentence (this isn't grammar class, okay?) that strings all these divine actions together. You might even want to turn it into a prayer, saying something like, "Lord, thank You that You …"

Let's go just a little bit further now. Considering what you underlined in the passage, what insights do they give you into God's …

- **knowledge of you?**

- **concern about you?**

- **understanding of you?**

- **interest in you?**

LORD, you have searched me and known me. You know when I sit down and when I stand up; you understand my thoughts from far away. You observe my travels and my rest; you are aware of all my ways. Before a word is on my tongue, you know all about it, LORD. You have encircled me; you have placed your hand on me. This wondrous knowledge is beyond me. It is lofty; I am unable to reach it.
PSALM 139:1-6

Who are some of the people in your life who relate to you similarly, who show concern for you and interest in you?

Search: to search out, to investigate

Observe: to scrutinize, sift, measure

Now that you've shown your work, let me show you some of mine. Two of the words that jumped out at me when I read these verses were "you have *searched* me" and "you *observe* [me]."

No one investigates or searches into something they don't care about. Nor do they observe someone in whom they take no interest. In order for our heavenly Father to be motivated enough to pay such close attention to us, He must first consider the object of His attention—*you*—extremely valuable and worthy of His detailed attention.

That's why the writer of this psalm—we believe it's King David—opened up by basically saying, sort of flabbergasted, "Why in the world would the God of the entire universe care this much about *me*?"

Can't you hear the awe in his voice, realizing not only that God could know so much about him, but also wanted to? God loved and took care of David more than even David loved and took care of himself. Do you see that? God not only possesses the capacity for having personal knowledge of you like nobody's business; He also, despite everything else on His plate today, prioritizes and desires knowing this much about you, His beloved daughter.

I'll wait here while you worship Him for that.

Here's a little extra space if you feel like writing your worship down. And I don't care how messy you get. Whether you use words or pictures, a ballpoint pen or colored pencils, scribble praises to Him all the way out into the margins.

Let's explore three important reactions that our study should elicit from us. First, I hope this whole concept of how God searches and knows you raises your awareness that He is everywhere, all around you, all the time. That's the main gist of what David said, beginning with verse 7. We need to know, really know, that God is with us. Always.

Turn to Psalm 139 in your own Bible and read verses 7-12.

Because of how deeply God sees and because of how inescapable His eye, what are some things He knows about you that no one else knows? (I realize it's a nosy question, but be honest. If you don't feel comfortable writing it here, please put it somewhere else. It's really important not to dodge it.) Think of what He, and maybe He alone, knows about your ...

Where can I go to escape your Spirit? Where can I flee from your presence?
PSALM 139:7

- **attitudes**
- **thoughts**
- **behaviors**
- **past**

- **hurts**
- **wounds**
- **fears**
- **failures**

Earlier you listed the names of people who care about you. What are some things about your private life that you wouldn't want them to know? How do you think they'd respond?

How would you respond if you found out certain things about them?

Yes, I want you to be aware and mindful—knowing—that as far as God's searchlight goes, "even the darkness is not dark to you. The night shines like the day" (v. 12). More than store surveillance, more than school security, more than cell phone cameras snapping pictures and posting them everywhere you go, you are never, ever, ever out of range of what God can see.

Here, then, is the second thing. And it's very important you don't miss this if you truly want to understand your identity. The promise of God's nearness to you and His knowledge of you is primarily designed to comfort you.

To comfort you.

God, how precious your thoughts are to me; how vast their sum is! If I counted them, they would outnumber the grains of sand; when I wake up, I am still with you.
PSALM 139:17-18

Look at Psalm 139:17-18 in the margin. No matter how often David may have squirmed at God's nearness and knowledge, what did his heart ultimately conclude about it?

"When I wake up, I am still with you" (v. 18). **How can you use certain parts of the day (morning, lunchtime, sunset, last thing before bed, etc.) as key moments for recognizing and being grateful for God's awareness of you?**

I'm sure you've felt that awful emptiness that sweeps over you when someone has found out about a part of your life you wanted to keep hidden. Maybe when they heard or discovered it, they responded to you with anger, or judgment, or rejection, or exclusion.

But God isn't like that. He isn't looking to catch you. He's looking because He loves you. He wants to help you. He wants to strengthen and encourage you. He wants to keep you from experiencing the shame and discouragement that goes along with being treated like or living like someone less than who you really are. He wants you comforted in knowing He has made you for incredible things, to be free and confident in Him, so you can actually be glad His eyes are seeing what nobody else sees. He wants you enjoying the benefits that come from living for Him, loving Him, and being exactly who He's created you to be.

Let this knowledge give you the assurance, too, that if you're in a situation where some secret things are being done to you–abuses that you've been told no one should ever know about or that no one cares about–God cares. He knows. He sees. You are not alone. Tell someone you trust, and trust that your heavenly Father has not forgotten you.

Then, one final thing before we close our day of study: an awareness of God's presence near you and His knowledge of you should convict you, the same as it convicts me. Conviction is when God's Spirit makes us feel uneasy about our sin and compels us to run from it as fast as we can. His all-encompassing camera angles should compel you and me to take seriously everything we do and think and say. We should want to honor Him because He is with us always.

His nearness *comforts* me because …

His nearness *convicts* me because …

THE VIEW FROM STREET LEVEL

*[He] has determined their appointed times
and the boundaries of where they live.*
ACTS 17:26

ONE OF THE FUN THINGS about my life is getting to travel to lots of different places. A few years ago, for the first time, my husband and I were invited to visit India. We loved every minute of it. No matter how hard we tried, we couldn't seem to digest all the exotic, incredible, overwhelming things we encountered (if you're not counting the loads of fresh baked naan we devoured! Yum.).

There is one thing about our visit that I will never forget. Dotted along the roadside every few miles in India are these idol worship stations. Everywhere. At first glance, especially at night, they're pretty engaging to see. Inviting even. The glitter of brightly colored carnival lights dancing in the cool night air pinpoint their locations. They're really something.

Idols blind us to our true identity.

But here's the deal. Idols, even the fancy and most festive ones, are still idols. And idols always blind people to their true identity. They cloud our vision of the true Creator. And whether they sit inside elaborately decorated shrines on an Indian thoroughfare, or fit comfortably inside the palms of our hands under our scrolling thumbs, or take up the majority of our time and energy, or assume a voice of authority louder than the voice of God in our lives, they disorient our view of both Him and ourselves.

What's an example of an idol in your life—something, someone, or even an idea or activity—that you've given more influence and control over your life than God?

What have been some of the effects you've observed, both in yourself and your peers, by giving so much power and importance to these things?

Our experience in India comes to mind whenever I read Acts 17. It's the story of Paul the apostle traveling through Athens, Greece, in the first century and becoming "deeply distressed." Let's see why:

Look up Acts 17:16 in your Bible. What caused Paul to become saddened?

Paul noticed one thing in particular that grabbed his attention. What was it (v. 23)?

Now read on to verses 24-25. List two or three of Paul's main points in the message he shared with the people of that region.

Read the scholar's remark in the margin. How do you see this same kind of idolatry evident in our culture today? Why do you think people are still so susceptible to it? Why so hungry for it?

Paul made a clear case about God being the sole Creator, the One who "made the world and everything in it." But not only did God do the big stuff–the whole universe stuff–He also did the little stuff. The you stuff. The me stuff. Even the timing and positioning of the you and me stuff.

Do you see it there in verse 26? How He "appointed times" for groups of people to exist? How He determined the geographical "boundaries" of where we would live? How He made every "nationality"?

In other words, not only are you not an accident, but even the specific setting, the circumstances, and the timing of your existence are not accidents either. Your heavenly Father meant for you to be here–in this family dynamic, in this city, inside your ethnic background, and living in this generation at this time.

One writer says of ancient Greece, "Divinity was to be found in the heavens, in nature, in humanity. The idea of a single supreme being who stood over the world, who created all that exists, was totally foreign to them."[4]

"From one man he has made every nationality to live over the whole earth and has determined their appointed times and the boundaries of where they live."
ACTS 17:26

Write about each of the following aspects of your life. How do you think God may have chosen you—a biblically literate, God-fearing warrior for Christ—to exist:

- in your skin? _____

- in your gender? _____

- in your family? _____

- in your school? _____

- in your church? _____

- in your city, state, and nation? _____

- right now—in this decade? _____

- in this generation? _____

In many ways, more than some people might admit, we can all feel out of place here sometimes, despite God's insistence that He put us here on purpose. I'm thinking of women I know (and of girls I knew when I was your age) who are light-years ahead of their peers in terms of their thought processes, ideas, and creativity. People tend to misunderstand them. It often leaves them feeling stifled and suffocated, as if they don't belong here. On the flip side, I've also met women who, instead of being up on the latest trends and fashions, are more emotionally connected with days gone by. They express their nostalgic nature with their vintage clothing or their bent toward simplicity or their romantic notions of a previous century. They, too, feel out of place, overwhelmed by fast-paced expectations that seem to clash with their innate design.

The truth of Acts 17:26 can set either woman at ease; it can set you at ease. You are not a mistake. You were meant to be here–with your temperament, in your birth order, with your unique personality and physical traits–to serve the purposes of God in this age.

A young man named Jeremiah felt this dilemma. Scholars believe he wasn't yet twenty years old when God said to him, "I chose you before I formed you in the womb; I set you apart before you were born. I appointed you a prophet to the nations" (Jer. 1:5).

Fill in the blanks from the four statements in that verse:

"I _____ you."

"I _____ you."

"I _____ you _____."

"I _____ you."

See Jeremiah's reaction in the margin to what God said of him—about whether Jeremiah believed God had made him exactly as He wanted him to be, exactly for the moment in history where God had placed him.

But I protested, "Oh no, Lord GOD! Look, I don't know how to speak since I am only a youth." JEREMIAH 1:6

Have you ever felt this way? If so, what made you feel inadequate to complete a task or job?

How have you allowed this sense of inadequacy to make you shrink back from being yourself?

When have you pressed on ahead anyway, confident in who God has made you to be and what He's called you to do?

Read how God responded in verse 7 to Jeremiah's denial in verse 6. How could you apply the Lord's words to a specific challenge you're facing today, in terms of feeling overlooked, out of place, misfit?

If you don't believe you can listen to what God has said in His Word about you—if you're a lot more tuned in to what you think, and what people think, and what the trends of culture seem to be saying—what your idols say—you'll almost always come to the conclusion that He made a lot of mistakes when He made you. He put you in the wrong body shape, burdened you with the wrong background, gave you the wrong skill set, entrusted you to the wrong parents, left you to deal with the wrong struggles, all within the wrong time frame.

Wrong, wrong, wrong.

You are who He made you to be, living where He wants you to be, when He wants you to be.

Chosen. Set apart. Appointed by God.

ROCKY ROMAN ROAD

> His invisible attributes, that is, his eternal power and divine
> nature, have been clearly seen since the creation of the world.
> **ROMANS 1:20**

SOME OF MY all-time favorite verses come from the book of Romans. Like these:
- "For the wages of sin is death, but the gift of God is eternal life in Christ Jesus our Lord" (Rom. 6:23).
- "Therefore, there is no now condemnation for those in Christ Jesus" (Rom. 8:1).
- "We are more than conquerors through him who loved us" (Rom. 8:37).
- "For I am persuaded that neither death nor life, nor angels nor rulers, nor things present nor things to come, nor powers, nor height nor depth, nor any other created thing will be able to separate us from the love of God that is in Jesus Christ our Lord" (Rom. 8:38-39).

But in order to get to all these life-changing passages in Romans 6–12 and to understand just how amazing the gospel truly is, we first need to go through Romans 1. And I'm telling you, it's not pretty. I still remember vividly, at age sixteen, the time when a well-known preacher visited our church and delivered a message on the second half of that chapter. It blew me away. And while I realize it's a tough, hard-hitting piece of Scripture, I know you can handle it.

We'll look at it in four quick bites. I'm going to write a portion of the passage and give you an opportunity to think through a few questions. As you read the verses, underline any key words or phrases that stand out to you. Let's go!

1. THE DANGER

> For God's wrath is revealed from heaven against
> all godlessness and unrighteousness of people who
> by their unrighteousness suppress the truth.
> **ROMANS 1:18**

What are some of God's truths that you see ignored, denied, twisted, or suppressed in today's culture? Even in Christian culture? Check the ones you notice the most:
- ☐ God creates each person as male or female.
- ☐ Sexual unity is designed for husband and wife.
- ☐ Jesus Christ is the only way to salvation.
- ☐ The Bible is the true, reliable Word of God.
- ☐ Church is a necessary part of the Christian life.
- ☐ Write down anything else you can think of: _____

What happens when people believe these truths to be lies, when we decide we want to live by another "truth"?

2. THE DESIGNER

> What can be known about God is evident among them, because God has shown it to them. For his invisible attributes, that is, his eternal power and divine nature, have been clearly seen since the creation of the world, being understood through what he has made. As a result, people are without excuse.
>
> *ROMANS 1:19-20*

Here are a few examples of God's attributes that are evidenced in creation. Match the physical observation on the right with the aspect of God it might reveal. There are no wrong answers.

power	math and science
grandeur	birds and birds' nests
faithfulness	otters and puppy dogs
joyfulness	sunsets and wildflowers
infinity	mountains and oceans
knowledge	stars and galaxies
provision	morning and evening
beauty	volcanoes and thunderstorms

For examples of occasions when God's wrath was revealed in the Old Testament, read about Noah and the flood (Gen. 6:5-7); Sodom and Gomorrah (Gen. 18:20-21); the Egyptian captivity of Israel (Ex. 7:1-5).

So according to the end of verse 20, "people are without _____" because God is revealed through what He's created.

To ignore, undervalue, or disrespect God's creation is to ignore, undervalue, and disrespect God Himself. With this in mind, consider two questions:

1. How does the way you treat or view yourself reflect your regard for your Creator?

2. Think of some of the other young women at your school who are different from you, either in interests or race or some other distinction. How does the way you treat or view them reflect your regard for their Creator?

3. THE DISCONNECT

For though they knew God, they did not glorify him as God or show gratitude.
ROMANS 1:21

According to the above verse, what two things do we sometimes neglect to do despite our knowledge of God?

1. _____   2._____

Rank the following words 1-6, with 6 being the strongest and 1 being the weakest, based on how they describe your feelings toward God's creation of you.

___ gratitude   ___ honor   ___ frustration

___ regret   ___ anger   ___ joyful

4. THE DARKNESS

Instead, their thinking became worthless, and their senseless hearts were darkened. Claiming to be wise, they became fools and exchanged the glory of the immortal God for images resembling mortal man, birds, four-footed animals, and reptiles.
ROMANS 1:21-23

"When Paul uses the word heart ('their senseless hearts'), he is usually referring to the most central part of a person, the hub of the soul. It refers to the thoughts, feelings, and ambitions of a person. This 'darkening' of the heart indicates mental dullness, emotional despair, and spiritual depravity."[5]

Verse 22 says they thought they were _____, but were _____.

Underline the key components of the quote in the margin. Now think about people you know or follow on social media who are not following God. Jot down some notes to discuss with your group about the evidence you see of "darkened" hearts in the following areas:

- **How we think (mental dullness, inability to reason or think clearly).**

- **How we behave (ambitions that don't line up with God's purposes).**

- **How we feel (unhealthy emotional states, lack of internal peace).**

- **How we relate to God (idolizing of nature or simply ignoring God).**

Okay, that was good work. Heavy, though, right? But do you remember just the other day when I told you to look not only for conviction when you read the Bible but also comfort? The same thing applies here. Even in Romans 1.

Of course, it's convicting. In fact, Paul explains in this chapter the horrible results that spiral down on any society that follows the patterns you've studied today. Three times he says God "delivered them over," letting them experience the consequences of what they wanted more than they wanted Him—sexual impurity, perversions, all kinds of terrible things. Read verses 24-31 and see for yourself.

Now look at verse 32, and let the gravity of this conclusion settle into your soul. Even though people know they deserve to die when they practice these things, "they not only do them, but even applaud others who practice them."

This is serious, sister.

And so it's worth asking: Are you participating in any of the negative, harmful things you saw in your study today?

If you're not personally engaged in them, is there any way you're applauding, celebrating, or "liking" others for doing these things?

How do the manufactured images of perfection that people create for social media affect your ability to live with contentment and gratitude?

"God delivered them over to the desires of their hearts" (v. 24).
"God delivered them over to disgraceful passions" (v. 26).
"God delivered them over to a corrupt mind" (v. 28).

And yet Romans 1 is also comforting. Because if all God wanted to do was pour down wrath and judgment on us, He has every right to do it. Instead, He seeks a loving relationship with us. He doesn't want to be hidden and unknown. He has chosen to reveal Himself to us through the beauties and intricacies of what He's created.

The takeaway from Romans 1 is not "God is mean." The takeaway from Romans 1 is that God doesn't want us living out the consequences of believing a lie. He wants us safe inside the freedom of our true identity.

So take your stand—even if it means standing alone, enduring the unspoken ridicule and resentment of your peers. Walk the narrow road. Make a personal commitment to honor God, be grateful for what He's created, and live a life that pledges allegiance to a heavenly Father who deserves your devotion.

HALF DAY

CONGRATULATIONS! You've come to the final day of the first week in your study. I know your days are filled with school, household chores, extracurricular activities, and all the other balls you're juggling. That's why I want the fifth day of each week to bring you here–to an invitation for you to rest in what you've already studied and simply cement the lessons God has been teaching you in your heart.

Also, I know very well you may need a chance to catch up in your study if you've fallen behind. I do that sometimes. (Well… a lot of times.) So take this day of study to choose a portion you may not have had time to complete yet, or simply take the opportunity to gather up the most important principles the Lord impressed upon you while you studied. This is how the Lord speaks–by putting a spotlight on certain principles or declarations in Scripture. If you sensed something personal and holy about a part of this week's study, write it here. Remember it. Treasure it. It's God's word to you, sis.

Yet LORD, you are our Father; we are the clay, and you are our potter; we all are the work of your hands.
ISAIAH 64:8

For we know, brothers and sisters loved by God, that he has chosen you.
1 THESSALONIANS 1:4

For we are his workmanship, created in Christ Jesus for good works, which God prepared ahead of time for us to do.
EPHESIANS 2:10

And on this first "half day," I want to give you a choice of three addresses that are each worthwhile places to go.

Choose only one of the three verses listed in the margin, and try thinking through these questions. No answers are wrong. Think freely and prayerfully.

1. **How could a person who didn't know or believe this truth about God make some really bad turns in life?**

2. **How would most people tend to react to this obvious hierarchy of authority and supremacy of God over us?**

3. **What would you expect to be the biggest differences about life on earth if this statement were not true?**

4. What is the Lord saying to you personally through this verse? How do you need to align your life with its message?

Truth matters. Even when it's difficult to accept. Even when it's difficult to understand. And the truth about you–the truth about me–is that God crafted us like a potter makes a work of art. He chose us for purposes known entirely to Himself. And He's made us capable, through His power at work inside us, to actually live a life of purity and love and worship and selfless compassion.

We can live our real identity.

We can do what God says we can do.

We can become who God says we can become.

Next week we're going to identify some of the complications that distort these beautiful truths, making them sound imposing, unfair, uncool, undesirable. But even with the trouble we cause ourselves, God never stops working with His "workmanship." He can still make this "clay" into exactly what He always had in mind.

But for now, let's close out this week in prayer.

> **Flip back through your pages from the last four days. Bring forward to this page some of the most inspiring, convicting, comforting things God showed you about His love for you in designing you uniquely and intentionally. Turn those thoughts and insights into a prayer—a prayer of thanksgiving.**

Week Two

STRUGGLES AND SOLUTIONS

PRESS PLAY

Use the space below to follow along and take any notes as you watch the video for Week 2.

In what areas of your life do you struggle the most with doing the right thing?

Sin is _____, and struggle is _____.

Consider your most common sin struggles. What desire is at the root of your sins?

You don't have to _____ yourself because you've been _____ by the Spirit of God.

Consider your own spiritual gifts. How can you use your gifts and talents to serve God and bring glory to His kingdom?

We're all _____ at the _____ of the cross.

You still are exactly who _____ says you are.

Define repentance in your own words:

EVERY CHILDHOOD SUMMER I spent at least a week, sometimes two, at Pine Cove Christian Camp. It was eventful for many reasons, but one of the highlights each year was the epic game of tug-of-war. Two dozen people would scamper toward either end of a long, thick rope, grasping its broad circumference with both hands. The stakes were high. A gargantuan, man-made mud puddle loomed in between.

So we corkscrewed our feet into the ground, anchoring a solid foothold. We widened our stances, bending our bodies into a sturdy crouch, lowering our center of gravity. And we waited… waited for the person in charge to blow that whistle, even as we tensed our muscles in preparation.

Ready? "Ready!!!"

The whistle would sound, and a fierce battle ensued. Pulling, bracing, leaning, screaming–whatever it took, to the end of our strength. Because we knew. We knew what losing meant. We knew if we let up for even a second, the momentum we could feel already building from the other side would yank us so far off balance that we'd never be able to recover. And that would be the end of it. Wet, messy, and disgusting.

Still, even if we lost, the annual summer tug-of-war was all in fun.

The everyday battle for your heart, however, is all-out war. And that's what you're up against, little sister–a constant tug-of-war of your own, except you've got a lot more at stake than just a muddy outfit.

All day long, there is an opponent on the other end of the rope, trying to muddy your soul and body. Sometimes you feel the tug stronger than at other times, but it's always there. Maybe just twitching. Bothering you. But then pressing. Pressuring you. Fighting. Swaying you. Pulling you away.

You want to live for Christ. You know what's right. You know what your best days have looked like. But today, at this moment, you feel the tug. Drawing you to accommodate a fleshly passion. Teasing you toward an unruly ambition. Pumping you full of doubts and lies. The moment you start thinking they're true–or when you simply stop proactively pulling in the opposite direction–that's when they drag you into the mud, where the tug always leads.

What if I told you, though, that one of the greatest Christians who ever lived experienced the same thing, the same kind of tug-of-war as you do?

Turn to Romans 7, and I'll show you.

Read Romans 7:14-24, written by the apostle Paul. I know it's a lot of verses, but I think you'll find them speaking your language.

Concentrate on verse 15. I've reprinted it here:

> For I do not understand what I am doing, because I do not practice what I want to do, but I do what I hate.
> *ROMANS 7:15*

I've never met anyone who didn't resonate with this verse. How would you paraphrase it? Go ahead, try putting it in your own words.

Describe an area of your own life where you want to do the right thing, but you're not doing it.

What do you "not understand" about this troubling situation?

How do you feel about yourself when you cave in and do things that, deep down inside, you don't even want to do?

Did you hear that? You don't even *want* to do it. You know it's bad for you. You know it'll only hurt you. And yet something is able to get you not just thinking about it but *wanting* it.

I know. It's crazy. And I bet I know exactly what you wrote as your answer. Know how I know? Because of what I wrote, when I answered it.

To realize you don't want to do something that has only ever caused you pain and trouble, and then finding yourself still wanting to do it, and then doing it, is maybe the worst feeling in the world. I get that. We *all* get that, okay?

So here's Part #1 to help you never feel isolated. It's not just you. It's all of us. The tug-of-war you feel raging inside you is a universal experience. Everyone feels it in some way. Every day.

But here's a very critical Part #2 for you to internalize and never forget. The tug does not define you. Hear me clearly: *You are not your struggle.*

> **Rewrite the italicized phrase, changing the "you are" and "your" to "I am" and "my."**
>
> _____ _____ not _____ struggle.

I meet so many women today who berate themselves severely, not only because of their sin, but simply because they are struggling against sin. They interpret the mere battle as a sign of failure or even a lack of salvation. They assume that just because they are being so powerfully tempted and attracted to a particular behavior, the temptation itself must be an indictment against their value and a confirmation of their identity.

> **Identify some of your biggest struggles in the following areas:**
>
> - **attitudes toward yourself**
>
> - **attitudes toward others**
>
> - **beliefs about God**
>
> - **selfish behaviors**
>
> - **sexual behaviors**
>
> - **avoidance behaviors**
>
> - **rebellious behaviors**

I'm not saying that any sins connected to these areas are nothing to worry about. (They are.) Although, if you've placed your faith in Jesus, the power to overcome them is already present within you. (More on that later.) But the struggle itself—do you hear what I'm saying?—the struggle itself does not make you "less than" in any way and does not dictate your identity. If God's Spirit would inspire someone like Paul to talk about the struggles he faced—in the Bible—you should feel the same freedom to express your own struggle without fear of judgment.

So don't cover it up. Don't equate it with guilt. Don't allow someone to discourage you by implying you've done something wrong merely because you have a difficult time with this, that, or the other. You are *not* your struggle. But do prepare to fight it, because the struggle can be won. Wrap your hands around that rope. And, by God's Spirit, tug! You were created for victory and abundance. But to see it start happening, you need to go to war. You need to start pulling.

> **As you think about the personal struggles you mentioned, how hard are you ready to fight back? It's time to declare war against your personal struggles. Write out your own resolution—your declaration of war—and include some of your best tactics, your best moves, in this fight. (Use some blank paper or your journal.)**

I can't tell you how many grown women continue to struggle with the grime of guilt, shame, fear, and lack of peace because they didn't decide to pull when they were your age. They thought they weren't strong enough to fight back. Or they were taught that they shouldn't even try because it wasn't worth the effort. Or they didn't think sin was such a big problem that it required this level of effort. Or they let their identity become so tangled up in their struggle that they defined themselves erroneously–already, at your age.

So today they're in their forties and fifties, yet in many ways they're just now getting started–learning who God has made them to be, learning what sin can do to them. They're just now discovering that life is a game of tug-of-war they can fight and actually win, as long as they line up on Jesus' side of the rope.

But you–I want you to discover it right here in Week 2. I want you understanding that you can sway the balance in the direction of God's truth. You can win, no matter your struggle. But it will require a consistent, deliberate effort.

This means war. And that means you. All the things that God has built into your identity are under fire. Your flesh and the nature of life on this planet make sure of it. But if you're tired of ending up face-down in the mud of poor decisions, against overpowering odds, the game is still yours to be won. In fact, the victory is actually already yours. Let's start mapping out a plan to add more strength and muscle where you need it the most.

> **Wrap up in prayer. Ask God to show you the sins and struggles that are working against you today, creating a sense of imbalance in your life. Ask Him to give you the courage to make the necessary changes that will move you toward victory in Jesus' name. Oh, and be sure to thank Him—ahead of time—for how He's going to help you turn this tug-of-war into a total win.**

PROBLEM CHILD

*Indeed, I was guilty when I was born; I was
sinful when my mother conceived me.*
PSALM 51:5

LAST WEEK we looked at the wonder of how God created you—internally and externally. "I have been remarkably and wondrously made," the Bible says (Ps. 139:14). Yes, you have. Yes, you are. But we ended the week with some strong hints at a problem that entered into this reality. *The problem is sin.* And while none of us likes to talk about it, we'd be dodging the truth if we didn't deal with it—as well as missing the "wonder" of what God has done, is doing, and will keep doing so that sin does no more damage to the amazing life He's given you.

Let's look at how this problem began. And along the way today, we're going to gather up a few really important theological terms I want you to keep locked away in your memory bank. In fact, I've given you three little banks on this page for you to write these terms on. I'll make the words easy to spot as we come to them. You won't need to read between the lines, I promise.

To get started, we'll need to go back to the dawn of time.

"No! You will not die," the serpent said to the woman. "In fact, God knows that when you eat it your eyes will be opened and you will be like God, knowing good and evil."
GENESIS 3:4-5

Turn to Genesis 3:1-7 and read it in your Bible. Pay special attention to verses 4-5, which are also in the margin, and answer the following questions:

1. **Who is the speaker in verses 4-5?**

2. **Who was he speaking to?**

How did he try convincing her to disobey God? (circle the best choice)
A. Play on her fears?   B. Cater to her hunger?
C. Get up in her face?   D. Appeal to her pride?

This is how Adam and Eve fell into sin. (So here's your first theological word: the *fall*. That's how scholars refer to this moment in the Garden of Eden—the *fall* of humanity.) (Write this term in Piggy Bank #1.)

Look now at another verse in the margin, the one from Romans 5. This is Paul writing, telling us about something extremely critical that happened when Adam and Eve took the serpent's bait.

Of the four phrases that make up this verse, underline the one that's the worst news for all of us today.

All the words in this verse are unpleasant, of course, but the worst part is that through one person's sin, "death spread to all people"–throughout all of humanity, for all time. And guess what, there's a theological word for this too: *imputation*. Not amputation, where something is taken away, but imputation, where something is added on. It's just a fancy way of saying that because Adam was head of the human race, his sinful nature spread like a cancer into the DNA of everyone who came after him. Including us. Sin has been *imputed* to us. It's part of us. It's stuck to us.

> Just as sin entered the world through one man, and death through sin, in this way death spread to all people, because all sinned.
> *ROMANS 5:12*

And this, dear friend, is why you and I and everyone living on the earth have such a struggle on our hands. The contaminant that has polluted every human being, no matter his or her race, gender, culture, or whatever, is called *original sin*. It means none of us comes into the world as a perfectly pure, innocent, blank slate, and then–oops!–we sinned, and we're out. We missed our chance. No. We had *no* chance. According to Scriptures like Romans 5:12 and others, we all start out as sinners. Before we're even born.

Look up Psalm 51 in your Bible, which is King David's prayer of repentance after he'd committed adultery with Bathsheba and then arranged to have her husband killed in an elaborate cover-up. (Psalm 51 is a good chapter to put a star beside and to pray your way through at times when you realize you've sinned against God.)

For now, look only at what David said in verse 5. What does it tell you?

Read the definition of *original sin* in the margin several times, thoughtfully. Write a two-sentence explanation of this concept in your own words below.

What evidence could you give (think about the behavior of babies and toddlers, if nothing else comes to mind) that proves human beings are born with original sin *imputed* on their hearts?

Have you noticed how, as children, we need to be taught how to share and behave and be happy for others? But not how to be selfish or dishonest or argumentative? Those last ones come rather naturally to us, don't they? That's because a sin nature resides in each of us, right out of the gate. It is general, not specific to certain people. It is universal, leaving nobody out. And it leads to sins of all kinds. Yes, you and I are all capable of all kinds of sin.

But today I want to isolate the one sin that's sort of the crux of all others. And we find it where we started, back in the garden of Eden. In fact, you already circled it in answer to a question I asked you.

The sin of *pride*.

Adam and Eve fell because of pride, because they exerted their own will and independence from God. The reason they disobeyed Him was because they wanted to be equal to Him in understanding. They wanted to know more than God. They bought the lie of their own self-importance.

And hear me on this:

Self-importance is always an enemy
to your true self-identity.

Whenever we elevate our own selves to the position that should be reserved for God alone, we take His authority and give it to another—whether to ourselves or to someone else. We then become guided by their directives, shaped by their influence. The result? We start living by the labels they give us instead of by the truth our Father declares about us.

Underline the three effects of pride listed in the previous paragraph.

How have you seen pride produce this result in your own life or in the life of someone you know?

Is there a specific area of your life where you've let pride replace humility? What would that area be? Make an effort to surrender it to God this week.

When you allow pride to rule, how does it affect your relationship with God? With others?

The *fall*, the *imputation* of sin, the fact that we're born with *original sin*— they're all ours because of pride. And if we want God's help in dealing with what sin has done to us, we must start by humbling ourselves before Him and asking for His help in getting back in alignment with Him, back in alignment with the truth.

And I promise to be here with you the whole way while we do just that.

End today's study by meditating on Romans 12:3. Write out a prayer committing yourself to humility and thanking Him for giving you the faith to believe that His way is actually what's best for you.

"This is true humility: not thinking less of ourselves but thinking of ourselves less."[2] RICK WARREN

By the grace given to me, I tell everyone among you not to think of himself more highly than he should think, Instead, think sensibly, as God has distributed a measure of faith to each one. ROMANS 12:3

THE SAME, ONLY DIFFERENT

*And some of you used to be like this. But you were washed,
you were sanctified, you were justified in the name of
the Lord Jesus Christ and by the Spirit of our God.*
1 CORINTHIANS 6:11

THE MISSISSIPPI RIVER runs more than 2,000 miles, flowing downhill
from central Minnesota, crossing into ten states, until it ultimately empties into the Gulf of
Mexico. It's a major waterway that basically divides the whole country in half—between "east
of the Mississippi" and "west of the Mississippi."

But check out this map of the Mississippi Delta, which covers mainly the southern part of
Louisiana, from New Orleans outward. And see how at the end of that mighty river, it branches
off into little fingers, called distributaries, fanning out into what's called a "bird foot" pattern. See it?

Our sin nature is like this. Each of us shares this main artery of original sin that runs straight
through all our hearts. But because we are unique individuals, the expression of sin—like a
river branching off into different distributaries—shows up differently in you than in me. That's
because Satan, aware of our specific personalities (the interests, desires, experiences, and
passions that God has placed inside us) tries taking advantage of what he knows about us. He
plays on our predispositions, even though they're not sinful in themselves, and matches them
with temptations that strike closer to our own hearts than they would to someone else's.

So while one person may struggle with substance abuse, another may struggle with telling the truth. One may be prone to stealing things, while another may go to extremes in her diet. A girl over here may be having a terrible time nursing anger against others, even as a girl walking right past her—poisoned by the same pool of original sin—finds her biggest battle in keeping herself pure from sexual promiscuity.

Same source; different expressions.

So let's dive into this. Look at 1 Corinthians 6:9-10 in the margin, and number the nine various components in this inventory of sinful behaviors.

Do not be deceived: No sexually immoral people, idolaters, adulterers, or males who have sex with males, no thieves, greedy people, drunkards, verbally abusive people, or swindlers will inherit God's kingdom.

1 CORINTHIANS 6:9-10

This is not a comprehensive list, by any means. It's only indicative of the pervasive activities and attitudes Paul saw expressed within the Corinthian community—although it does look startlingly similar to what we'd observe in the twenty-first century, doesn't it?

I've already asked you to write down the sinful temptations, like these, that cause you the greatest tug-of-war. Why is it so important that we know where we are the most vulnerable and susceptible to temptation?

Now choose some categories from this list (or name others) that you actually *don't* struggle with. Write those down, too.

How does it make you more compassionate and less judgmental about others and their struggles, knowing that they're actually dealing with the same root issue as you?

Sin can be expressed in a myriad of different ways. But pinpointing and calling out the specific manner in which your sin nature usually shows itself in your life is the beginning of victory. And victory is what we're chasing here.

A seventeen-year-old at my church told me recently that she finds herself easily entangled in gossip when she's with a certain group of chatty, negative friends. Noticing this pattern, she monitors her comments closely and even excuses herself when she can tell the conversation is getting muddy. It feels like a little victory, every time.

What proactive measures do you need to take to be victorious in an area where you struggle?

Underline the first sentence found in 1 Corinthians 6:11.

See, Paul's reasons for writing 1 Corinthians 6 was not to rant against sin, trying to make people feel bad. He did it to show the difference in the life of someone who's in relationship with Jesus, as opposed to one who's detached from Him. He wrote it to say, because of the power and grace of God, believers can lay hold of a new identity marked by new behaviors.

Our struggles with sin cause us all kinds of trouble, yes. But they can't keep us from access to a divine remedy. You can come as you are to Christ with total confidence that, even if the struggles continue, you can break your losing streak to them. You can "come as you are" but (this is the great part) not "stay as you are."

Jesus' entire ministry was marked by this approach. He made people feel accepted–many who rarely felt accepted by anyone else–yet He never left them the same afterward.

Choose three or more of the following examples, and read the passages that accompany them, noting how Jesus practiced a "Come as You Are" but "Don't Stay as You Are" approach with the people He encountered.

	Come As You Are	Don't Stay as You Are
Woman at the Well	John 4:16-17	John 4:23-26
Adulterous Woman	John 8:3-6	John 8:10-11
Man with Leprosy	Matthew 8:1-2	Matthew 8:3
Zacchaeus	Luke 19:1-7	Luke 19:8-10
Thomas	John 20:24-25	John 20:27-28
Peter	Matthew 26:31-33	Luke 22:31

"Some of you used to be like this," Paul said. This is who you were. This is how the sin in your life has uniquely expressed itself. But this is not who you are anymore. God has offered you a solution to your biggest problem. And that solution is found "in the name of the Lord Jesus Christ" (1 Cor. 6:11).

So this is an important day. A well-rounded study of identity would be incomplete without spending time (as we've done) on the nature and pervasiveness of sin. But no matter what you've admitted about the sin in your life during this week–no matter how defeated or shackled you may feel–I come with good news that changes everything.

Look at Romans 5:17-18. I've reprinted it here from a version called the Amplified Bible, Classic Edition.

For if because of one man's trespass (lapse, offense) death reigned through that one, much more surely will those who receive [God's] overflowing grace (unmerited favor) and the free gift of righteousness [putting them into right standing with Himself] reign as kings in life through the one Man Jesus Christ (the Messiah, the Anointed One). Well then, as one man's trespass [one man's false step and falling away led] to condemnation for all men, so one Man's act of righteousness [leads] to acquittal *and* right standing with God and life for all men.
ROMANS 5:17-18 (AMPCE)

These two verses encompass so much of what we've been exploring. What do they tell you in terms of:

1. The effect of Adam's sin

2. The effect of Jesus' gift

I mean, your identity is incredible, simply because you've been created by God, right?

But sin.

Adam's sin. Adam's sin became your sin. Then your sin became your unique sins. It's left our identity tarnished.

But God.

Our God. He's brought you a gift. And inside that gift–the gift of Jesus Christ–is an identity that can completely transform what sin has done to the identity God wanted for you.

FROM DEATH TO LIFE

When you were dead in trespasses...
he made you alive with him.
COLOSSIANS 2:13

MY COUSIN WYNTER was not just my cousin but actually one of my closest friends. She was more like a biological sister than a distant relative. She was the best friend who joined me at the movies for an impromptu girls' night or for dinner at a local restaurant. If something funny or scary or difficult happened in my life, she was one of the first people I'd call to laugh about it, celebrate it, cry over it, or talk it out. We took vacations together, raised our children together, and even mapped out our plans for the future together.

Which is why it came as a complete shock when Wynter's heart just suddenly stopped beating on July 24, 2018.

She'd been completely fine earlier in the day. In fact, she'd been sitting in my living room, braiding her girls' hair, getting them ready for a summer outing. After finishing all four, she'd lain down and taken a little nap. Her last phone message to me was at 5:00–making plans with me for the following day.

But at 6:15, she was gone.

She was 38 years young.

Several days later, as family and friends gathered, four of us women were tasked with going ahead of everyone to the funeral home to make sure Wynter's body looked presentable before the viewing at her service. I don't know how else to say it: she still looked radiant, even in her casket. A beautician had coifed her hair, and a makeup artist had meticulously cared for her face. She was wearing a gorgeous dress and dainty jewelry.

But here's what you already know, as much as I wished on that day that it wasn't so. No amount of hair styling or makeup or nice clothes or accessories were able to put breath back into my sweet friend's body. She wouldn't be calling and leaving messages on my phone anymore.

Wynter was dead.

And death cannot be undone by outward adornments and modifications.

Look up the following verses, and write their common theme below.

Ephesians 2:1

Ephesians 2:4-5

Colossians 2:13

Considering what you've read about my cousin Wynter, as well as the verses you just looked up in your Bible, what spiritual principle can you derive regarding the limits of outward remedies on our spiritual condition?

Spiritual death means you are separated from life with God. Your human spirit is darkened, deadened, disconnected from the Father, and no amount of behavior modification can undo it. You may be able to improve in areas where you've been practicing sinful behaviors. You may be able to tweak some of the influences and relationships and lifestyle patterns that contribute to your struggles. But none of it will change the condition of your spiritual reality.

It's no different than applying makeup to a corpse.

Real change–the type of change that lasts–begins from the inside out.

So let's talk about this change, this rebirth, this *regeneration*. (Notice a good definition of regeneration in the margin.) Then at the end of today's study, I want us to pray together so you can open your heart to God, inviting Him to create this kind of change inside you.

"Regeneration is the process by which God implants new spiritual life, His very life, in the heart of a sinner who believes on Jesus Christ for salvation."[3]

Consider the implications of *regeneration* as expressed in each of the following portions of Scripture. Draw a line to connect the passage with the correlating principle.

John 3:1-3	New creation
Romans 6:4-5	Rebirth
2 Corinthians 5:17	Resurrection

See, this is not just about patching things up, trying a little harder, or copping a better attitude. All of that is fine, but none of it can make you come to life. In order to step into the full identity that you can claim by receiving Christ as your Savior, you and I need God to do something for us that we could never do for ourselves. We need Him to change us from within.

Here, let me try explaining it like this: I love hot, salty, buttery popcorn. It's my favorite snack, and I could eat it all the time. Recently I learned something about popcorn I'd never heard before. Inside every kernel of popcorn is a microscopic dot of water. When you place a pot of uncooked popcorn on the cooktop, the heat penetrates the shell and begins warming up that dot of water. The liquid water transforms into steam, the steam builds in intensity, and soon it creates a growing amount of energy on that popcorn shell. When the outer shell is no longer able to handle the pressure that's pushing out from the inside, it explodes. Then all of a sudden, the tiny hard shell becomes a perfectly popped piece of popcorn.

That's sort of how God changes your and my life, too. When we pray to receive Christ, He places His Holy Spirit inside of us, like the water inside of popcorn. His Spirit's presence in our human spirit awakens our deadened souls from their spiritual slumber, and as His life grows in us, we change into something new and different.

We still possess our old sin natures. We still have some of the same old struggles. But because we have His Spirit inside–God's resurrection power inside–He gives us the desire to be holy and the capacity to no longer cave to the whims of our flesh.

Do you have that?

Would you like that?

Hopefully you've already received the gift of God's Spirit by confessing your sins and placing your faith in Jesus. Perhaps, though, you haven't. But here's my question: As we keep moving through this study–and as you can see, there's a lot of it left to go–do you want to just read about what *could* be? Or do you want to actually *experience* it?

I want you living out what can truly happen in your life because of what Jesus wants to give you as the solution for your sin.

So here's a prayer I'd like you to pray with me. If you're already a Christian, you can pray these words as a recommitment of your allegiance to Jesus and as an expression of gratitude for the changes He's made possible in your life. But if you know you've never put your belief in Christ, I'd love if you'd join me without any fear or doubt in God's desire to empower you. Don't just say these words. Believe them.

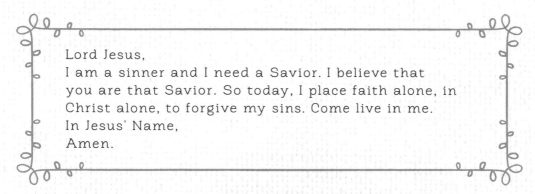

Lord Jesus,
I am a sinner and I need a Savior. I believe that you are that Savior. So today, I place faith alone, in Christ alone, to forgive my sins. Come live in me.
In Jesus' Name,
Amen.

That's how death comes to life, my friend.

You're reborn. You're regenerated. You become a new creation. You're a child of God. This is your new identity.

And now we get to explore it all together.

If you made a decision to receive Jesus Christ as your Savior today, please tell your group leader, your parents, your pastor, or someone you know and trust. This is so amazing! And I'm incredibly excited for you.

OLD HOUSE, NEW ME

From the beginning God has chosen you for salvation through sanctification by the Spirit and through belief in the truth.
2 THESSALONIANS 2:13

OUR FAMILY recently moved into a new house after searching for one for more than a year. We looked at so many houses that I can't even remember them all. Some were old; some were new; some were both old and new at the same time.

One of these old/new houses had been built nearly three decades earlier but had undergone significant renovation. Walls had been torn down so rooms could be widened and reconfigured. The living areas were fresh, modern, and all Joanna Gaines-like. Kitchen appliances were state-of-the-art. The bathroom amenities had never been used. The whole place looked brand-spanking-new… on the inside.

The outside, however, told a different story. While the owners had incorporated a few upgrades, most of the house's original exterior had been left untouched. Window moldings were crumbling. Visible stains marked many of the white stone accents. The driveway contained lots of broken and cracked bricks, chipped from years of use.

So while the interior looked really nice–like new!–the exterior still needed a lot of work.

Read James 1:21 in the margin, paying special attention to the highlighted portion. What does James say still needs to happen, even in the life of someone whose soul has been saved?

Therefore, putting aside all filthiness and all that remains of wickedness, in humility receive the word implanted, which is able to save your souls.
JAMES 1:21 (NASB, EMPHASIS MINE)

The beauty of being a believer in Christ is that He makes us totally brand-new on the inside. We're not only changed; we're *exchanged*. The old is thrown out; all-new stuff goes in. But your new identity is still contained inside an old house (an old body) riddled with sin. Your *spirit* is renewed, but everything else, including your mind and will and inclinations and emotions, still needs a lot of renovating.

But no worries. God knew this would happen. He knew He'd be starting out on a renovation project–not to fix the unique features of your body or the unique passions that live inside your soul, but rather to mold and use those unique characteristics as instruments of His glory. It's the parts that *don't* reflect your identity that need the touch of His newness. And He has a solution for these, thanks to the same Holy Spirit who's now living inside you.

Turn to 2 Thessalonians 2:13, and search it thoroughly for the theological word that describes the Holy Spirit's work in believers. Is it:

A. salutation   **C. sanctification**

B. sanitization   **D. saturation**

Using the definition in the margin, fill in the blanks to complete what this important term means.

Sanctification means being _____ into the _____ of _____.

Sanctification is the process by which we are molded into the image of Jesus, so that we begin to have the mind, attitude, and actions of Christ.

The Holy Spirit's desire and responsibility is to begin the transformative work of renovating you from the inside out. This "gift" that God has given you means He's committed Himself to making incredible, noticeable changes in your life, where you actually become more and more like Jesus. A little more all the time.

But God your Father knows, like all good parents know, that just giving His children something and then doing all the work for them is not how we kids learn. Unlike salvation, which is *all* God's work (ain't nothing we can do to make that happen), sanctification is something He invites us to cooperate with Him in doing. So for this next part, you and I need to put on our hard hats. We're about to get our hands dirty. Your God has come down to this job site called *(insert your name here)* _____ to work directly with you in getting this renovation project started. It's going to be difficult, but hear me now: "He who started a good work in you will carry it on to completion until the day of Christ Jesus" (Phil. 1:6).

Are you ready? Let's do it.

Each of the following verses reveals cooperative efforts of ours that support the Spirit in His sanctifying work.

Therefore, brothers and sisters, in view of the mercies of God, I urge you to present your bodies as a living sacrifice, holy and pleasing to God; this is your true worship.
ROMANS 12:1 (EMPHASIS MINE)

Do not be conformed to this age, but
be transformed by the renewing of your mind,
so that you may discern what is the good,
pleasing, and perfect will of God.
ROMANS 12:2 (EMPHASIS MINE)

Therefore, ridding yourselves of all moral filth and the evil
that is so prevalent, humbly receive the implanted word,
which is able to save your souls. But be doers of the word
and not hearers only, deceiving yourselves.
JAMES 1:21-22 (EMPHASIS MINE)

And don't grieve God's Holy Spirit. You were
sealed by him for the day of redemption.
EPHESIANS 4:30 (EMPHASIS MINE)

Rewrite the highlighted portions in your own words:

1.

2.

3.

4.

5.

6.

Now think about how you can cooperate with God's Spirit in achieving these specific directives. Fill in the blanks next to the following statements with the corresponding number of the principle you just described.

_____ Intentionally and categorically refuse to participate in behaviors that dishonor God. And refuse to laugh at or applaud the actions of others that are out of alignment with His truth.

_____ When God's Word is taught to me, I will not just hear it. I will do it.

_____ Remind myself every day that my body is not my own. It is God's temple to be used only for His purposes and objectives.

_____ Realize that God's Spirit lives within me. Therefore, I don't want to do anything that would hurt or offend Him or would work against what He's seeking to accomplish in me.

_____ Be intentional and diligent about reading, studying, and memorizing God's Word, so I can absorb His truth into my heart.

_____ Take careful notice of the things I think about, making any changes necessary to be sure I'm thinking like a Christian.

Which of these are the easiest for you to do?

Which are the most difficult? Why?

Circle one that's particularly difficult for you, and make it a matter of specific prayer. Consider talking with someone who can help you figure out a strategy to make this action a new habit in your life.

Hey, great job on all that. Even just filling out this section, I know, has taken a lot of work. But this is good. This is a good thing. A challenging thing, but a good thing because these practices (and many others like them) will change your entire life. They will accelerate your growth and enable you to live in a way that lines up with your new spiritual identity. And best of all, you can count on the Holy Spirit to be your guide and biggest cheerleader the whole time. He loves helping you change. He loves it when the hard work you're doing actually starts showing up on the outside of the house, where everyone can see what you and He have been up to.

It's a process. It takes time. You won't be perfect until you see Jesus face to face, so you'll be working on it your whole life. In fact, we all are. But nothing—I promise you, _nothing_—feels as good as knowing you're working in tandem with Him, watching Him fix stuff that's been broken and messed up for so long, seeing yourself becoming what He says you've already become on the inside.

You know what? That hard hat looks really good on you.

HERE WE ARE AGAIN at the end of another week. I'm so proud of you for making it this far.

This has been a difficult week, I think. But a valuable one. Maybe this week you even laid down all your resistance toward God and said, "You know what? I want to beat my struggles." You asked His Spirit inside you by putting your trust in what Jesus has done for you, and you're on your way now to fully living out your identity in Him. Or maybe you reaffirmed or recommitted yourself to letting Him lead you. Either way, the trajectory of your life is headed in a direction worth going. And you're only getting started.

Today, on this "half day," I want to share a quick story with you. First, though, I'd like you to look quickly at a couple of verses.

Turn to 2 Corinthians 3:17-18. What does Paul say in verse 17 that the Holy Spirit is able to give us? _____.

And according to verse 18, He does it by *transforming* us.

He takes things that once dominated us, and He transforms them "from _____ to _____" until they actually become something He can use for good. He frees us to serve Him with all our hearts, making the most of the identity He's given us.

Can you think of anything that might fit this description from your own life?

When I was your age, I dealt with an area of weakness that, when combined with a fierce independent streak that often recoiled against authority and boundaries, could turn into sin in an instant. It was my mouth. I often heard people say, "Priscilla talks too much." And they were right. I did. Talked out of turn. Talked before thinking. Talked with the wrong tone. Talked at the wrong time. Just talked. Talked too much. And because of how many times I was told to "Stop Talking!" (or certain words to that effect), I began to internalize my desire for communicating as negative, as bad. So I began consciously trying to make myself an entirely different person–quieter, more internal and less verbal–despite how sullen and unhappy it made me. I didn't realize then that being a communicator wasn't the problem. Disobedience was.

Gratefully, my parents were discerning. They wisely separated these things. They knew when to give me consequences for the trouble I caused with my lack of self-control, like when I disobeyed the rules at school. But they did something else. They also made intentional efforts to help me redirect those negatives into a positive possibility. They told me if I would surrender my unique propensities to the Lord, and if I would let the Holy Spirit govern my tongue–to think before speaking–He could make something good come from the way the Lord had obviously made me.

Well, here I am today, serving God in a capacity where my talking–lots and lots and lots of talking–is one of the primary ways He uses me. The Holy Spirit, working from inside my struggle, renewed my mind, molded my character, and matured me, helping me live out the uniqueness of my identity through the uniqueness of my struggle.

> **With this perspective in mind, can you imagine any of your current struggles as being not all negative, but perhaps the uncommon seeds of positive opportunities?**

> **How could you imagine Him transforming a specific struggle into something useful and positive? Freeing and fruitful?**

It's just one little example of how incredibly exciting this journey into your God-given, Jesus-bought, Spirit-enabled identity can be. Will you join me again next week so we can take it a little further? Hope to see you then.

Week Three

VITAL SIGNS

PRESS PLAY

Use the space below to follow along and take any notes as you watch the video for Week 3.

_____ is tied very closely to your level of _____ with the Father.

The more you know _____, the more clear view you will have of _____ .

Intimacy breeds a more clear view of your _____.

What makes it difficult for you to sustain an abiding relationship with Jesus?

We make time for whatever our _____ are.

How can you build a stronger friendship with Jesus starting right now?

What does practicing the presence of God look like for you?

WE HOMESCHOOLED our three sons for a few years, and it was great. Although to some it can seem like a permission slip for sleeping late, not showering, and generally goofing off (which we totally did sometimes), we worked really hard.

True, the time savings that come from not having to go through the hectic morning routine and driving to a school building every day does allow for a creative, less rigid, more flexible schedule. We enjoyed the relaxed pace we could incorporate into most days. Plus, the boys were able to join us when we traveled, which gave them firsthand experiences visiting different parts of the country, even different parts of the world–opportunities they may never have had otherwise.

But I was serious about their schoolwork. The "work" part was not negotiable. I always made sure they were learning the basic skills they would need for their future. Nor did they get to skip tests, although the tests I chose to give them weren't the kind I handed out and then graded at my desk. Mostly, I set them up with an online resource where they could measure their own progress by testing themselves.

Turns out, the Bible was preaching the value of self-testing long before we could create our own test on a website.

What's the real purpose for the tests you take at school? (I suppose I'll accept answers related to "torture," but try to keep it positive, okay?)

What makes self-testing different from classroom tests?

Look up and match each verse with the corresponding reason that's given for why God ordered this self-test.

Lamentations 3:40	Eliminate the moving targets of comparison
2 Corinthians 13: 5	Target your relationship with God
Galatians 6:4	Get yourself back on target

Some Christians believe a life of faith shouldn't require any tests. Why do you think that is?

It's true that the salvation God offers us through Jesus Christ is unconditional. The Father considers His Son's death on the cross as suitable payment for our sins when we place our faith in Him alone (not ourselves) as our only hope of becoming righteous before God. Nothing more is required to redeem us than what Jesus has already done.

Read Colossians 2:14 aloud:

> He erased the certificate of debt, with its obligations, that was against us and opposed to us, and has taken it away by nailing it to the cross.
> *COLOSSIANS 2:14*

Isn't that incredible? His payment for your sin, if you've accepted Him as your Savior and Lord, is safe and secure. "The one who has the Son has life," the Bible says, just as "the one who does not have the Son of God does not have life" (1 John 5:12). You don't flunk out of relationship with Him. His life in you is forever. In fact, your eternal life actually starts *now*.

But it's easy to doubt that these promises God has made are true, especially when things get tough. It's difficult to always feel confident that He won't one day take back this invitation He's given us that says we can live with a new identity fully, freely, and without fear.

We said some words; so what?

We prayed a prayer; so what?

Give an example of when someone followed through on a promise to you. How did you know he or she would honor the promise?

How do you think God might use tests to reveal Himself and His promises to us?

Through faith, we know God's promises are true—by believing "that he exists and that he rewards those who seek him" (Heb. 11:6). Faith is always key to your relationship with Him, right from the start and all the way through. But God understands your heart and mind. He knows you and me so well, in fact, that He has mercifully decided to give us a way to see that what He's said is true. That's what the self-tests we're going to explore this week are for.

They're proof that He's alive in you. They're evidence that He's changing you. They're meant to encourage you and give you confidence that your new identity in Him is true and is working for you.

So are you ready for a little self-testing?

Here are five questions. Five statements, really. And, of course, it's important that you be completely honest as you answer them. Remember Galatians 6:4? "Let each person examine his own work… and not compare himself with someone else"? Because what's the point in that? In comparing? What's the use of trying to look better than others? This test is for *your* good. It's designed to help you, not compare you, definitely not to fail you. The only thing any of us should be looking for here is the truth.

So grab your pencil, scoot up close, and …

> **Underneath each statement, circle your best, most authentic estimate (on a scale of 1-10) for how well you think you're doing in all five of these areas.**
>
> **I have a progressively increasing desire to obey God. Doing what He says is what I truly want to do, all the time, more and more.**
> 1 —— 2 —— 3 —— 4 —— 5 —— 6 —— 7 —— 8 —— 9 —— 10
>
> **When I sin, I feel the inner conviction of the Holy Spirit. Then I quickly want to repent, to change, to live in a way that honors God.**
> 1 —— 2 —— 3 —— 4 —— 5 —— 6 —— 7 —— 8 —— 9 —— 10
>
> **I value and expect God's discipline when I disobey Him. I know I'm not really getting away with behaviors that are not right.**
> 1 —— 2 —— 3 —— 4 —— 5 —— 6 —— 7 —— 8 —— 9 —— 10
>
> **I genuinely love other people, especially other believers. I treat them well and care about them, even if they've treated me poorly.**
> 1 —— 2 —— 3 —— 4 —— 5 —— 6 —— 7 —— 8 —— 9 —— 10
>
> **I intentionally and consistently seek to know God more intimately and remain close to Him through prayer and His Word.**
> 1 —— 2 —— 3 —— 4 —— 5 —— 6 —— 7 —— 8 —— 9 —— 10

There you go.

Now we'll be coming back to these statements, so make a note of these page numbers. Throughout our time together this week, we'll be exploring the biblical backgrounds for these foundational statements. And before you move on, discuss your answers with your group. Let's be honest and willing to share where we are and where we're going to need some help.

And here's why we're doing this kind of work in a study that's based on *identity*.

Your identity is rooted in God. He designed you. You've been created in His image, and–if you've received Christ by faith into your life–you've been recreated into a new person who reflects the identity of God's Spirit who now dwells within you. So the better you know *Him*, the more you actually know *yourself.* See how that works? The more you grow in your walk with Him, you actually live out more and more of the truth about who you really are. You grow into your new identity.

When your own new identity in Christ starts growing, you are transformed. It reveals what's now possible for you, the potential in you. It's a beautiful and powerful thing. Your God-given identity starts flowing through your own unique design, so that His heart and purposes are seen through you.

And that's what we're after. That's why I declared this a test day. But as you can see, it's the kind of test I hope you'll actually look forward to revisiting and retaking, because none of it is deviously planned to trick you or trip you up. It's only designed to broaden your horizons, to clear things up, to bring both the inside and the outside of your life into such harmonious alignment that you can be *you* all day–your living identity–like maybe you've never experienced before.

Don't think of it as taking a test. Think of it as learning to be your best.

TO KNOW HIM

You are being renewed in knowledge according
to the image of your Creator.
COLOSSIANS 3:10

I INVITED a new friend over to my home earlier today for a visit. I'd only met her on one previous occasion. We'd spent about an hour together that first day. Mostly the small-talk variety. We were involved in a meeting, a business-type setting. Hello, my name is… you know, that kind of thing.

But today when she came over, we were able to settle in for a longer, less formal conversation. And I found out a lot more about her.

She's originally from Alabama. She and her husband, along with their children, moved here to Texas about four years ago. After talking with her today, I now know some things about her hometown, her parents, the church where she grew up, the parts of her life and the work she's doing that she's enjoying the most right now, the places where she finds fulfillment. We had a really good time today, talking about tons of different things. I wouldn't be surprised if we start getting together a lot more.

> **Do you have anybody you feel that way about? Someone you'd like to know better? Who is it? (Maybe you should do that.)**

Well, if you had asked me before today whether or not I knew this woman, I'd have said, "Yes, we've met. She seems like a really nice person." But if you ask me whether I know her now, my answer would carry an extra layer of meaning. And if you were to ask me the same thing six months from now, my answer might contain far more information than you ever wanted to know.

This is the purpose of spending time together—deepening friendship and building intimacy.

> **Turn to John 1:43. What's the name of the person Jesus met that day?**

Turn to Matthew 10:2-3. Do you see this same person's name again? How well do you think he and Jesus probably knew each other by then? Why?

Now turn to John 14 and read verses 1-9. By the time of this conversation between Jesus and His disciples, it's pretty late in His ministry. Immediately after chapters 14-17 (which is commonly known as Jesus' "farewell discourse"), you'll see Him betrayed by Judas and headed soon to the cross. His time on earth was nearly over.

Look at verses 8-9 in the margin. Underline the first sentence that Jesus said to Phillip.

I want you to look up several verses from earlier in the book of John. Match them to what Jesus (the Son) said in that verse about His relationship with His Father.

John 5:19	No one has seen the Father except the Son.
John 5:23	The Son always does what pleases the Father.
John 6:46	The Father and the Son are one.
John 8:16	The Son only speaks what the Father has told Him.
John 8:29	The Son and the Father make judgments together.
John 10:30	The Son does only what He sees the Father doing.
John 10:38	People should honor the Son just as they honor the Father.
John 12:50	The Father is in the Son, and the Son is in the Father.

All right, think back now to John 14:9, the verse you underlined in the margin. How could Philip have been with Jesus "all this time" and not understand the connection between Son and Father?

"Lord," said Philip, "show us the Father, and that's enough for us." Jesus said to him, "Have I been among you all this time and you do not know me, Philip? The one who has seen me has seen the Father. How can you say, 'Show us the Father'?"
JOHN 14:8-9

Have your parents or teachers ever expressed frustration with you about something that "I've told you and told you!" and yet you haven't seemed to really get it? Why is that true? What are some of the reasons you've either resisted or not understood what they've been saying to you?

John actually wrote five books out of the twenty-seven in your New Testament: John (the Gospel of John), 1 John, 2 John, 3 John (three letters to early believers), and also Revelation.

John, who was one of Jesus' closest followers, wrote his Gospel with the intention of helping people meet Jesus and place their faith in Him for salvation. But meeting someone and knowing them are two different things. Knowing them takes spending time with them. We're not supposed to know and understand as little about Jesus as we did when we first met Him. After being around Him for a while, we should know Him more and more, better and better … better all the time.

In fact, John–this exact same guy–wrote a later book of the Bible called First John (1 John), and one of the main themes throughout that book is the idea of *knowing* God. So that's where we're going to live this week, in 1 John, and I hope you come to love it as much as I do, learning more of what it means to know Him. Since your spiritual identity as a young godly woman is inextricably tied to who your Father is, knowing Him better and more closely should be your continual goal.

But, today is not a test day. You've done enough good Bible study for one day, I think. So let's just close with a story.

If you've seen the movie *Overcomer*, you're familiar with the young character named Hannah who discovers that her father–a man she never knew, a man she'd been told was dead–is actually alive. He's sick and in a nearby hospital. Through her cross-country coach, Hannah finds out her dad would like to meet her–if she has a desire to meet him. Maybe you remember that emotionally intense scene where she sees her father for the first time. She's overwhelmed. She can't even speak. She's not quite ready for what the shock of it does to her, and she rushes out of the room.

But as time goes on, Hannah's life begins to change. Her perspectives, priorities, and behaviors shift, and she refocuses her attention on getting to know her dad. She doesn't want to waste another minute being disconnected from this person whose DNA she shares. She goes to visit him in the hospital as often as she can. And interestingly, the more clearly she knows him, the more fully and accurately she begins to view herself. She starts to understand her strengths, her weaknesses, her uniqueness–her whole life, in fact–in an incredible new light.

The same is true for you, as well. The more you know of your heavenly Father and the more intimate your connection with Him becomes, the more fully you begin to understand who you really are and what you're really capable of becoming. First you know Him through salvation, but then you start to know Him through ongoing fellowship. And in knowing Him better each day, you move toward understanding, accepting, and living out your God-given identity and potential.

End today's lesson by asking God to reveal Himself to you more and more each day. Ask Him to let your friendship be ever-growing in intimacy for the rest of your life.

THAT THING YOU DO

> This is how we know that we know him:
> if we keep his commands.
> *1 JOHN 2:3*

I'M EXCITED about studying with you today. Let's get to it!

I've printed an extended passage from 1 John 2 in the margin of your book. I'd like for you to read it through, not once, but twice. If you're interested in doing more, I'd even suggest you pull up an online Bible and read this same passage–1 John 2:3-6–in another translation of your choice.

This is how we know that we know him: if we keep his commands. The one who says, "I have come to know him," and yet doesn't keep his commands, is a liar, and the truth is not in him. But whoever keeps his word, truly in him the love of God is made complete. This is how we know we are in him: The one who says he remains in him should walk just as he walked.
1 JOHN 2:3-6

List at least three words or phrases that stand out to you from these verses, and tell me why they're intriguing or curious to you.

What would you say is the one-word takeaway from this passage?

Fill in the following blank: If we say we know God, we should _____ Him.

Yes, *obey* Him. Evidence that a Christian is truly growing in their knowledge of Him is that they will have an ever-growing commitment to *obedience*.

Do you remember the self-test I asked you to take at the beginning of this week? Flip to page 62 and read the first three statements.

In light of today's theme, write down any connection you find between these three statements.

Were you able to pick up on the fact that all three test statements orbit around a single, common theme?

- The first one talks about *obedience*.
- The second one talks about getting *back* to obedience, after you've disobeyed.
- The third one talks about what God does to help you *stay* obedient.

A growing commitment to obedience is one of the vital signs of a Christian. It's an indicator of whether or not you're growing and maturing in your walk with Him and are coming to know more about Him. It's not only an indicator of your spiritual growth, but is also the key to realizing and accessing your newfound identity in Him.

Here's why: Disobedience leads only to insecurity and fear and a lack of internal peace. It creates distance between you and the Father and leaves you confused, angry, disoriented, and defeated. It disrupts the flow of your friendship with Him, which in turn cuts off the intimacy you need for giving you a clear view of your identity. This is why the enemy wants you hung up in rebellion and disobedience. He wants to be sure the freedom, vibrancy, and authenticity that God offers stays outside of your spiritual reach.

This highlights an important question: Can someone be disobedient and be a Christian at the same time?

Look at 1 John 3:9 in the margin. Circle what he says Christians do not do.

Wow, that's a pretty startling statement. A Christian "does not sin." A Christian is not even "able to sin." Let that verse sit with you for a moment. Do you feel any sort of concern or worry as you think back to the numbers you circled on those first three questions?

I've been a Christian since I was seven years old. Although I was young when I committed my life to Christ, I believed what I was saying when I asked Jesus to be my Savior, and I was truly saved. But I've been anything but perfect in the decades since then. My teen years were punctuated by bouts of rebellion against my parents' rules. My college days were a collage of questionable choices. And even though I straightened up in my twenties, I continue to make lots of ridiculous mistakes and missteps. Now in my forties, I *still* struggle against sin today. Sometimes I let pride take over. Sometimes I embellish the truth. Sometimes, I've been slow to obey the clear leading of the Holy Spirit in my life. I'm a Christian, and yet, I still sin.

> Everyone who has been born of God does not sin, because his seed remains in him; he is not able to sin, because he has been born of God.
> *1 JOHN 3:9*

How about you?

Does your behavior make 1 John 3:9 a complex truth to understand? How?

If we say, "We have no sin," we are deceiving ourselves, and the truth is not in us.
1 JOHN 1:8

Now read 1 John 1:8 in the margin. How do these words strike you as curious, even contradictory, in comparison to 1 John 3:9?

You and I will never be perfect on this side of eternity, okay? Anyone who thinks they are perfect, or even attempts to be, is fooling themselves. Listen, perfectionism is a crippling vice that, if you let it, will leave you frustrated and discontented for decades to come.

Loosen your grip on that unattainable goal right now. Let 1 John 1:8 set you free. It provides a radical truth about your identity that can change the course of your whole life. If you can really get this—if you can cement it in your heart and mind right now in this season of your life—I guarantee you'll see an enormous progression in your relationship with God and in the freedom you'll experience as His daughter for years to come. Now let's explore the meaning of 1 John 3:9 further, so we can grasp what the author is saying to us.

Look at 1 John 3:9 again. Why does the passage say a believer no longer sins?

Fill in the blanks: "Everyone who has been born of God does not sin, because _____ _____ _____ _____ _____."

This "seed" that God has deposited within you is the life of His Spirit that pulses at your core. And this "seed" is the part of you that is "not able to sin." This "seed" is what is yours because you've been "born of God." This "seed"—God's pure and righteous Holy Spirit—can never produce sin in you. It's impossible.

So are you perfect? No. You're not perfect. But—oh, little sis, don't miss this: *there is something perfect inside you.* And so at the core of who you are in Christ, John is right—you cannot go on practicing sin. The seed you carry around with you is incapable of sinning. This is why you can live freely and victoriously. This is why sin doesn't have the power to control you anymore. This is why you do not have to cave to temptation and live below your standing as a daughter of God.

God's seed—His perfect seed—is in you.

Now, because you are still in your flesh and live in a fallen world, you'll never be perfect on this earth. You'll make mistakes and you will sin every time you fall to the enemy's temptations. Make no mistake about it, every time you "walk according to the flesh" instead of walking "according to the Spirit" (Rom. 8:4) you will succumb to sin. But…

> **What does Galatians 5:22-23 say is able to grow in your life like "fruit" on a fruit tree, simply because there's a seed inside you that can only produce this kind of crop?**

When you're living in the light of your perfectly new identity, sinlessness will be your overarching lifestyle. Instead of habitual defeat, interrupted only by short bursts of victory, you can experience long, consistent stretches of obedience and abundance.

The "seed" makes all the difference—the seed that "remains" in you.

You can do it, girl—not because you're perfect, but because the perfect seed of God is in you.

> For this is what love for God is: to keep his commands.
> And his commands are not a burden, because everyone
> who has been born of God conquers the world.
> *1 JOHN 5:3-4*

Take the burden of perfectionism off yourself. It's too heavy a load for you to carry. There has only ever been One who is perfect. And it was Jesus. The Perfect One has already come and He paid the price for you. He's the only one who could shoulder that kind of weight and responsibility. So let Him carry it. Let Him carry you. Leave the job to Him. Rest, pursue Him, and watch His life empower yours.

LOOK ALIVE

This is the message you have heard from the
beginning: We should love one another,
1 JOHN 3:11

TWO OF JESUS' FRIENDS—sisters Mary and Martha—sent word to Him that their beloved brother, Lazarus, was gravely ill. They expected and hoped that Jesus would come quickly and do something to keep him from dying. Yet to their dismay, He waited four days before arriving. By that time, Lazarus was already dead.

Jesus cried when He found the two sisters distraught in their grief. (Proof that Jesus cares when we hurt. "Jesus wept," the Bible says in John 11:35). But then He did something amazing. He went with them to their brother's graveside and ordered the onlookers to remove the stone from the mouth of the tomb. "Lazarus, come out!" He shouted. Immediately the dead man roused awake and stood there alive!

Then Jesus said something else—something that's not quite as well remembered, but I mention it today for a specific reason. Lazarus had walked out of the tomb wrapped up like a mummy in his grave clothes. And when Jesus saw him, He said to the crowd again, "Loose him, and let him go" (John 11:44, NKJV).

Because the clothes of death don't suit the living.

Lazarus was alive! And his outside needed to show it.

We know that we have passed from death to life because we love our brothers and sisters. The one who does not love remains in death.
1 JOHN 3:14

The verse in the margin says we can know we're alive in Christ if… (fill in the blanks)

"We know that we have passed from _____ to _____ because we _____ our _____ and _____."

We spent yesterday looking at the first three questions from your self-test, the ones that dealt with obedience and how it reflects your new identity. Today we turn to Statement #4 on page 62—the one that speaks about how you feel toward other people who share your faith in Christ.

What was the number you ascribed to yourself for this area?

Who's an example of a Christian you've treated poorly, either in the past or maybe even right now? Write a little about the circumstances surrounding that.

Can you think of someone at church who's been unkind or dismissive of you, yet you've deliberately tried to express the love of Jesus to him or her? What's a specific way you've done that?

According to 1 John 3:14, the believer who doesn't interact with others on the basis of love "remains in death"—kind of like staggering around in the ill-fitting, stench-filled clothes that a person is buried in, even after they've been resurrected and given new life. Like Lazarus, we need to aggressively tear off anything that still represents the domain of darkness and death—the domain that our salvation has delivered us from—because of the One who "made you alive with him" (Col. 2:13).

> And when you were dead in trespasses and in the uncircumcision of your flesh, he made you alive with him and forgave us all our trespasses.
> *COLOSSIANS 2:13*

Since God is love, it follows that those of us whose identity is now aligned with His nature would express His love to others. That's why your ability to love the unlovable is yet another confirmation of what God is doing inside your heart.

Turn in your own Bible now to 1 John 3, where he uses several other illustrations to teach us the importance of living out our identity of love. In verse 15, for example, what horrible action does John specify as being equivalent to hate?

How does the dramatic connection between these two actions—hate and murder—make the seriousness of this issue more apparent?

In comparison to how God loves, what are some less-than-loving attitudes you've taken toward others—attitudes that are probably a lot closer to hate than you'd like to admit?

One of the clearest examples of this dynamic is the relationship between Cain and Abel, the first brothers of the first family. John referred to these siblings in verses 11-12 to make his point about how Jesus wishes we would treat our spiritual brothers and sisters. Travel back with me to Cain and Abel's story in the Old Testament, and let's see what we can learn from them.

Turn to Genesis 4:3-8. After you've read it thoroughly, answer the following questions:

What caused the problem between these two brothers (vv. 3-4)?

How did God respond to each brother (vv. 4-5)?

What was Cain's emotional reaction to God's different responses toward the brothers (v. 5)? Extra credit: What other emotional responses do you think Cain might have felt, which fueled his fury and despondence?

What important message do you think God was trying to express to Cain (vv. 6-7)?

What did Cain do to his brother (v. 8)?

Remember what Jesus taught about the connection between anger and murder?

> "You have heard that it was said to our ancestors, Do **not murder**, and whoever murders will be subject to judgment. But I tell you, everyone who is angry with his brother or sister will be subject to judgment."
> *MATTHEW 5:21-22*

The emotions people pass through on their way to murder don't *seem* as if they would end up resulting in such drastic actions. But the root of death is embedded inside those emotional stages, even in feelings like anger, which is fueled at some level by hate.

Each of us has felt anger in our hearts toward someone else. Whenever a person betrays us, or embarrasses us, or uses us, or disappoints us, our natural tendency is to lash out in anger— or at least build protective emotional walls around ourselves, in hopes of staying barricaded from additional hurt.

You won't go to jail for "crimes" like that, but by continuing to allow anger and hate to fester, by living in a state of bitterness and animosity toward someone, you're committing murder in your heart, the Bible says.

And I don't think that looks like you … like your *identity*.

You're alive now. So take off the clothes of death as fast as you can!

Your true nature—your new nature—expresses the powerful love of God. It can melt away the hardened, calloused places in your own soul, then spill outward in kindness and compassion toward people who may not even deserve it.

> **End today's lesson by carefully considering whether or not you're harboring hate in your heart toward anyone. Even if it's someone who is no longer in your life, ask the Lord to give you courage by His Spirit to offer the forgiveness that will free you from the bondage of hate.**
>
> **Thank your heavenly Father for delivering you from the domain of death, and ask Him to give you the courage to take off any spiritual attire that doesn't align with your new life in Him.**

Dear friends, let us love one another, because love is from God, and everyone who loves has been born of God and knows God. The one who does not love does not know God, because God is love.
1 JOHN 4:7-8

REMAIN IN HIM

> "I am the vine; you are the branches. The one who
> remains in me and I in him produces much fruit,
> because you can do nothing without me."
>
> *JOHN 15:5*

MAYBE YOU'VE HEARD someone ask this rhetorical question: If you were
to be put on trial for being a Christian, would there be enough evidence from your life to
convict you?

**What is your personal response to that question? Does your lifestyle give evidence of
your faith?**

I suppose this question could seem unnecessary. Should we really need to prove it? Aren't we
forgiven and accepted and safe in the arms of Jesus? *Of course* we are, if we've put our faith
and belief in Him. But what we've been discovering this week is that God wants to give us
everyday assurance that this faith is for real–that this identity of ours changes us into people
who are different than we've been before.

**So having thought through the first four self-test statements, what difference do you see
already in how you feel about the two vital signs we've discussed so far?**

　　1. **Your obedience.**

　　2. **Your love for others.**

What does the evidence from your life reveal about your intimacy with God?

Today we're going to finish up by looking at the last test entry from page 62, which says: *"I
intentionally and consistently seek to know God more intimately and remain close to Him through
prayer and His Word."*

What do you think it looks like to "intentionally and consistently seek to know God"?

What evidence do you see of this Christian quality in your life today?

Thinking of days when you may struggle with your desire to pray or spend time in your Bible, what would you identify as the main things that contribute to that lack of zeal?

So now, little children, remain in him so that when he appears we may have confidence and not be ashamed before him at his coming.
1 JOHN 2:28

John really liked using the Greek word that is translated "remain" in 1 John 2:28. (Underline that word in the verse found in the margin.) He actually used it forty times in his Gospel and twenty-seven more times throughout first, second, and third John. And with so much emphasis, it must be of critical importance to anyone who wants their life brimming with evidence of their faith and their new identity in Christ.

This particular Greek word is *meno* (pronounced "MEN-oh").[1] Today I'd like to explore it more closely with you by using one of the study techniques we did together earlier, where we searched for other places in the Bible that contain the same original word. One of the most memorable of these places, in regard to *meno*, is found in John 15.

Turn to John 15:1-5. After reading this passage, see if you can locate four instances where *meno* is used. (Hint: they're all in verses 4 and 5.)

Did you find them? Did you see the word "remain" in that passage? Perhaps your Bible used another word: "abide." Either way, it's the same original word *meno*, which implies a confident, ongoing, organic connection. In literal terms, it means to hang out or to stay. Like at a slumber party with some of your friends or at Starbucks® over Frappuccinos®.

In fact, since I've gotten us all in the mood for a tasty beverage, I think I'll use one of my favorites as a way of plunging a little deeper into what *meno* means and what it produces. I enjoy ending the day with a tall, steaming mug of jasmine green tea with a dollop of honey. I put the tea bag into the mug while the kettle is warming on the stove. Then when it's reached the boiling point, I pour the hot water over the bag.

I like to let the bag *remain* for quite a while, allowing all the flavors to filter into the water. Sometimes I even leave the tea bag in there the entire time I'm drinking it. The longer I let it *abide* in the water, the stronger the tea becomes.

But I've noticed not everybody drinks their tea this way. I've met people who, instead of letting the tea bag remain there, dip it in and out of the water. Maybe it's a nervous habit. Or maybe they don't like their tea to start tasting too strong.

Using my observations about hot tea, what are some of the characteristics of a person who remains in Jesus?

What about the person who is up and down, in and out, in his or her walk with God?

The strength and depth of your intimacy with Jesus will depend upon your commitment to *meno*–to hanging out with Him in prayer, in His Word, in His church, and also in the place where He's planted you to flourish. If you dip in and dip out–sometimes seeking Him, sometimes not; sometimes attending church, sometimes not; sometimes praying, sometimes not; sometimes obeying, sometimes not–you'll find your faith weak and watered down, not potent and flavorful.

Go back to John 15:4-5, where our Greek word *meno* appears a handful of times. What's the illustration John uses to describe what it looks like to abide in Christ?

What part of this illustration represents Jesus?

What part represents you as a believer?

Which one of these terms would best describe the proper relationship between Jesus ("the vine") and the believer ("the branch")?
  A. Conflicted   C. Connected
  B. Conquered   D. Contrived

One theologian describes it as "mutually abiding"[2]—you in Him and He in you. Do you see that? *His* job, which He is always faithful to do, is to stay connected with you from the vine, to continually strengthen you and provide spiritual nourishment to you on your journey toward spiritual maturity. *Your* job is to stay connected to Him—not just for a day, not just for the eight weeks that you and I are studying together, but throughout all the ebbs and flows of your life.

And you can do it because Jesus *remains* in you to empower you to *remain* in Him.

Listen, throughout your life you should expect that your relationship with God will look and feel different. Some stages will allow for a more traditional "quiet time" experience, while other seasons will require you to "practice the presence of God" as you hum your favorite worship song and get ready for basketball practice. In one stage of your life, your work hours may allow for you to attend Wednesday night Bible study at your local church, while the job you have in another season may require you to work odd hours that conflict with traditional service times. In any case, you can still remain connected to Him. Never let guilt or frustration about how you remain connected to Him ruin the sweetness of your relationship with Him. It doesn't matter how you do it, or what it looks like in any particular season. You are His and He is yours—ready to meet with you, His daughter, throughout your day and in every season.

So even when your prayer life feels dry, pray. *Remain* there. When you don't see much point in reading your Bible, or when you feel your mind starting to wander, get reconnected. *Abide* there.

Abiding requires consistency and faithfulness over an extended period of time. And as you deliberately cling to Him, your life will begin bearing more and more of the fruit He wants to produce through you.

Don't disconnect from the life-giving root system of Jesus—through sin or apathy or distraction or whatever leads you to pull away. The nutrients you need for growth are all in Him.

Thank God today for His commitment to remain connected to you. And then evaluate how well you're remaining connected to Him. Recommit to the disciplines that keep you connected even when your passion may be waning.

IF YOU'RE ONE of those girls who just cannot be happy unless you've made a perfect score on everything you turn in—relax and remember that a perfect test score is not what we've been aspiring for this week. We've been measuring *growth*. We've been measuring *progress*. All you should want to do is know God better today than you knew Him yesterday. That's a passing grade in my book.

To close our week, I want to highlight again the important aspect of your identity we read about in 1 John 3:9, because it is a game changer. Look at it in the Amplified version of the Bible. Underline the portions of this expanded version that speak to you the most.

> No one who is born of God [deliberately, knowingly, and habitually] practices sin, because God's seed [His principle of life, the essence of His righteous character] remains [permanently] in him [who is born again— who is born from above— spiritually transformed, renewed, and set apart for His purpose]; and he [who is born again] cannot *habitually* [live a life characterized by] sin, because he is born of God *and* longs to please Him.
> *1 JOHN 3:9 (AMP)*

God's Word brings us *conviction* (which is a good thing), and God's Word brings us *comfort*, remember? We need both. This verse stirs conviction, for sure. But your Father knows you. He knows you're not perfect. And that's why, along with conviction, He also comes strong with the comfort.

Grab your Bible and turn to 1 John 1. Starting with verse 9, read all the way into chapter 2, stopping with verse 2. (Don't worry, it's only four verses. And once you see them, you'll be really glad you know them.)

Write down the most affirming, comforting thoughts that God tells you in each verse:

1 John 1:9

1 John 1:10

1 John 2:1

1 John 2:2

Sister, you live in a sinful body, in a sin-contaminated world, warring against a real enemy who will always tempt you toward sin and away from your true identity. God lets you confess your sins, and He is faithful to forgive them. Amen. And yet, because of what Jesus has done and because of what you've believed about Him, something has changed between you and your sins. Your battle against sin is no longer a guaranteed loss. You may still *want* to sin. But you don't *have* to sin. You're not controlled by sin. You can have victory over sin. You're not powerless against it, unable to resist caving to it.

In fact, that's one of your signals, your vital signs. One way to recognize that you're really starting to know God better is an ever-increasing distaste for sin. *Conviction* meets *comfort* meets *confidence* because you're seeing the difference your new identity can make.

First John 3:9 is right. Sin should *not* be the normal pattern of behavior for any true believer who's growing in their relationship with God. And though He'll always give comfort when you fail, He can actually give you something even better: confidence for the fight.

Sin is not for you. Sin is no good for you. And when you're living your real identity, you'll see for yourself: sin is *not* you.

> **End this week with a firm resolve to walk away from any patterns of sin that are incongruent with your new identity. Ask the Lord for His courage to make the difficult choices that will give you victory.**

Week Four

WHO YOU
ARE

PRESS PLAY

Use the space below to follow along and take any notes as you watch the video for Week 4.

You are who _____ says that you are.

What kinds of lies does the truth of God counteract?

How do you begin to transform and renew your mind, so that you see your real reflection? List a few practical steps you can take.

The only thing that _____ your mind and literally changes your _____ from the inside out is God's Word.

We've got to go ahead and bring our _____ _____ to the _____ of God's Word.

Consider the purpose of your last social media post. Was it done in light of your true identity or from a place of insecurity?

LET'S TALK

REMEMBER THE MOVIE I told you about last week? I was so honored to have the opportunity to play a school principal named Olivia Brooks in the film, *Overcomer*.

Olivia, in her leadership position, is naturally responsible for the educational well-being of all her students, but she takes a more personal interest in one particular girl, a young ninth grader named Hannah. She's aware of some of the unique challenges Hannah is facing. And one day at school, while happening upon an opportunity to engage with her in private conversation, Olivia clearly sees that Hannah is really hurting about something. It's not one of those moments where she needs help with math or with any of her other school subjects. Olivia can tell she's needing a deeper, internal transformation.

Soon their talk begins drifting toward spiritual things. And as Hannah opens up about some of her own struggles and questions, the tender-hearted principal explains the gospel to her and asks if she'd like to accept Jesus as her Savior. In one of the sweeter, more touching moments of the film, Olivia clasps hands with Hannah, and the two of them pray together for her to be born again. In that moment, Hannah's identity is transformed. She becomes a new creation.

A lot of things in Hannah's life are still the same at that point. Her struggles, frustrations, and circumstances don't magically change. Just because she's become a Christian doesn't mean all her problems go away. But because of Jesus, *she changes*. And because of the change in her, a lot of things become very different. (The same is certainly true for you, as well.)

After Hannah accepts Jesus, Ms. Brooks asks if she'll do her a favor.

OLIVIA: *There's a book in the Bible called Ephesians. Will you read the first two chapters, and write down everything it says about who you are as a believer in Jesus Christ?*[1]

Hannah says she'll do it. And she does.

Well, now, I want to ask you, little sister…

Will *you*?

I'm asking you to read two whole chapters of the Bible and write down everything it says you are as a believer in Jesus Christ. (*Is Mrs. Priscilla really going to ask me to read two whole chapters of the Bible?*)

Yes, I most certainly am.

Listen, these next two weeks are the heart of our study. And these first two chapters of Ephesians are absolutely crucial to understanding the enormity of your new identity. On most days during the next two weeks, yes, we'll typically highlight and spotlight only one particular passage or concept. But today, I want you to soak up the rich words of Ephesians 1–2.

I did this exact same exercise myself not too long ago.

I got together with five other people, and we read Ephesians 1–2 out loud to each other. It was actually fun. And extremely eye-opening. Whenever one of us heard something that indicated our new identity in Christ–like *adopted, forgiven*–we yelled it out for all the others to take note and write it down. We had a great time, mining the treasures of this incredible passage together.

That's what I want for you, too. Since I believe you want God's Word to speak deeply to you, and that you want to experience something new and fresh and powerful from the Lord, I believe it's my responsibility to challenge you to get your heart totally prepared to hear what He wants to say. *His* words, not my words, are the ones that'll change your life.

So here's my assignment to you for today:

> **Read the first and second chapters of Ephesians aloud. (In a group of two or three, if you'd like.) As you read, watch carefully for anything Paul specifically says about who you are as a follower of Christ. When you think you've found one, call it out and record it on the journaling lines I've provided for you on the next page.**

Ephesians 1:3, for example, talks about something you *have* ("every spiritual blessing in the heavens in Christ"). That's an enormous benefit you now possess, and next week we're going to focus more tightly on what you *have* and what you've been *given*.

But today and throughout this entire week, I want you concentrating primarily on who you *are*–like in verse 4, where Paul says:
- God "chose us in him" (*You are chosen.*)
- In order that we can be "holy" (*You are holy.*)
- And "blameless in love before him" (*You are blameless. You are loved.*)

See how it works?

Start with these four and continue to add new statements as you come to them. Not every verse will contain one. Sometimes you may not spot one for several verses. You may also see some of them repeated. But read through and see how many you can identify.

I know you're up to this task. See you on the other side.

"I am chosen." "I am holy." "I am blameless." "I am loved."

_____

_____

_____

_____

_____

_____

_____

_____

_____

_____

_____

_____

_____

_____

_____

_____

_____

_____

You did it! You made it through. I am really, really proud of you.

Now listen, I wouldn't be surprised if reading these two chapters and working to find these "who you are" statements felt pretty difficult. It's like taking up a new sport or exercise plan. It's *not easy* at first.

Which statements have you heard and believed in before reading them today?

Were any of the statements new to you? Something so big and wonderful that you had never fully understood them before?

Which statements do you struggle to believe the most?

Perhaps you also feel like, even though you've read it, you didn't understand a lot. That's okay, too. I don't expect you to grasp every nuance from one reading. (Hey, I've read these chapters I don't know *how* many times, and I'm still learning new things as God shows them to me.) But having gotten yourself basically familiar with what's written here, it's going to make the rest of these two weeks just burst alive for you. By the time we start drilling down into various spots along the way, you'll realize, *oh yeah! I remember that!* The soil of your heart will already be tilled so God's Word can really stay planted, because of the up-front investment you've put in.

Ephesians 1–2. They're going to be one of your favorite all-time places in the Bible to go, from here on, all throughout your life. And to think your love and mastery of them perhaps started right here.

Right now.

Today.

ADOPTED

In love He predestined us to adoption.
EPHESIANS 1:4-5 (NASB)

IN JULY 2013, my friends Stephen and Jill Kendrick endured one of the toughest plane rides of their lives. Not only were they on a l-o-o-o-n-g flight from China to the US, but they were traveling with their newly adopted, two-year-old daughter, Mia.

And to put it mildly, Mia was not happy. *NOT.* Happy.

Here's how Stephen describes it:

> Throughout the long twelve-hour flight, she was screaming and crying loudly. She didn't know what was going on, who we were, or where she was going. She had no idea we were actually rescuing her from an orphanage in a communist country and taking her to a new, loving, happy home in a free country.
>
> Though she owned almost nothing in China, she would now have her own bed, her own clothes, and lots of toys waiting for her. She had no known parents in China, but now she'd have two loving parents, four siblings, four wonderful grandparents, and a ton of cool cousins ready to welcome her with open arms. In China, as an orphan, she likely faced a lonely and dangerous future. But now, as part of our family, her future was bright and safe.

This little two-year-old girl's entire life was being reframed. In amazingly good ways. She'd been given a brand new identity–as Mia Kendrick–with her status changed from "orphaned" to "adopted." Imagine if she had known how much different, how much better her life was going to become. She would've been smiling and celebrating the whole way home. Not freaking out.

When have you been Mia, afraid of not knowing or understanding what lay in store for you?

Can you think of any ways you've fought and resisted your heavenly Father, who's "adopted" you as His own daughter?

What's made it difficult for you to accept or understand all the good things His adoption of you entails?

Mia's story is our story—except that our adoption story, like everyone's story when they become a part of God's family, is actually a million times better. We're not just talking about getting a new room and more attention paid to us; we're talking about being given eternal life in a heavenly mansion that Jesus has gone to prepare for us. We're not just talking about being saved from an orphan's existence; we're talking about being snatched from the fires of hell, if not for God's pure-grace decision to love us and come looking for us.

And if our lifestyle is anything but gratitude and celebration—in stunned relief at what we've been spared, and in awe of what we've been given—we must not truly realize what an incredible gift and opportunity we have.

Did you put "I am adopted" (or something like that) on your journal page when you read Ephesians 1 and 2? If not, go back and add it now.

God "chose" you—"before the foundation of the world," the Bible says (Eph. 1:4)—to be His child. In love He adopted you "according to the good pleasure of his will" (Eph. 1:5). He handpicked you to experience all the benefits that come from being a part of His family. So no matter the ways you may have been rejected, even orphaned, you can know you're part of a family with a loving Father who is looking after you and your future.

You are a daughter of the most high God!

Are there any personal circumstances you've faced that make this truth especially meaningful to you?

What are some decisions you've made or actions you've taken in the last few weeks that you might have done differently if you'd realized *who you are*?

I don't know if you're someone who's experienced a lot of rejection in your life or not. Maybe some of the people you thought would love you have

For he chose us in him, before the foundation of the world, to be holy and blameless in love before him. He predestined us to be adopted as sons through Jesus Christ for himself, according to the good pleasure of his will,
EPHESIANS 1:4-5

treated you like you don't really matter to them. Maybe you've spent a lot of your life feeling like an outsider, orphaned and left to flounder. I'm sorry. And I'm certainly not minimizing the pain you've endured because of it.

But let the truth of who you are in Christ wash over you today—the beauty and bounty of your true identity in Him.
- You've been *chosen.*
- You've been *adopted.*
- You are *beloved* of God.

In fact, turn to Ephesians 2 right now, and look again at the difference God has brought to your life—from who you *were* to who you *are.*

"I am alive."
"I am saved."
"I am seated in heavenly places." Those are a few more "who you are" statements you can add to your list, if you haven't already.

Your version of the Bible may be different from the one I'm using, but I think you'll be able to fill in these blanks as close as possible from the way the verses sound in yours.

"You were _____ in your _____ and _____." (Eph. 2:1)

You used to live "according to the _____ of the _____." (Eph. 2:2)

"We were by nature _____ under _____." (Eph. 2:3)

"At that time you were without _____ ... without _____ and without _____ in the world." (Eph. 2:12)

But even with all these marks against you, He made you " _____ with _____. ... You are _____ by _____!" (Eph. 2:5)

"He also _____ us up with him and _____ us with him in _____ _____ in Christ Jesus." (Eph. 2:6)

You are "in Christ" now that you've been adopted by God. And this new spiritual status of yours becomes the grid through which you filter your entire life. Who you are in Him outshines all the other labels that may identify you—whether negative labels that have previously crippled you, or even positive labels (good things) that are a part of who you are.

Let me speak to this point briefly as we wrap up. As an African-American woman, I am made in the image of God. Neither of these aspects of my identity is an accident. I am an illustration of the multifaceted creative genius of my Father. He made me this way. He wants me this way. Being a member of God's family does not negate or dismiss these identifying characteristics of mine, any more than Mia's becoming part of the Kendrick family did away with her Chinese ethnicity. Instead, my uniqueness equips me for unique kingdom ministry. God will use my uniqueness as instruments to express His heart to the world around me.

I can be unapologetic and proud of my ethnicity and my gender. These are positives. And yet, I must be careful not to allow any aspects of my humanity to eclipse my identity in Christ. My allegiance is to Him. This means that I submit my full self to His truth, so that I am conformed into the image of Jesus Christ. If any agenda or movement connected to these demographics I embody does not square with biblical truth, God's standard prevails. I choose my identity as His daughter as my best and highest good.

What are some similar aspects of your own God-given identity that, although positive and good, must be kept in alignment with God's truth—a daughter of the King?

Think of a time when you've seen or heard people choosing to support an agenda associated with their physical demographic over their allegiance to God's truth as His child. What have you observed to be the outcome of that?

We're not all the same, but as believers in Christ, we're all part of the same family. Why? Because we've been adopted. We converge underneath the umbrella of our holy kinship, where we find unity, acceptance, and freedom in our true, beloved, adopted selves.

End today's lesson by personalizing the prayer below and speaking it out loud to your Father.

Lord, thank you for making me exactly as I am. I praise you for these aspects of my physical uniqueness: _____ and _____. I submit my full self to your authority because I want to be conformed into the image of your son, and I want every part of me to be used for your glory. Thank you for choosing me and adopting me into your family. I am yours. Amen.

RENAMED

To the faithful saints in Christ Jesus.
EPHESIANS 1:1

MY FRESHMAN YEAR of high school, I transferred to a public school from the private one I'd attended since kindergarten. I was excited about it. Feeling a bit mischievous, I decided to embark on an experiment in my new environment. Instead of telling people that my name was Priscilla, I thought I'd just introduce myself by another name, a nickname I'd made up for myself.

My childhood friend Nicole was one of the few people I knew who went to this school, and I brought her in on my plan. She wasn't too crazy about it, but she agreed to play along. So on the first day, each time she'd stop to introduce me to a group of her friends, she'd turn to me and say, "This is Pri—I mean, uh," her voice trailing off for a moment. She'd shoot me an inquisitive look to make sure I wanted this charade to continue. *Yes,* I smiled in response. *Yes, I did.*

Before the day was out, I'd been officially stamped by my new nickname. In fact, there wasn't a single teacher, student, or member of the school administration who did not refer to me by that name when I graduated four years later. I even had it monogrammed on my sports uniforms and my letter jacket.

I had renamed myself.

Think about my illustration in light of our study on spiritual identity. Have you ever done something like this? Even if you didn't tell anyone else, is there a name or label you've given yourself?

Is there a label or description that other people in your life have stamped on you, and over time, it's become a part of how you think of yourself?

How does that name affect how you feel about yourself? Does it impact your behavior? How does it influence some of the relationships and choices you make?

I eventually ended up learning a valuable lesson about self-naming and labeling, right back there in high school. I learned it from my mother, and she made sure I never forgot it.

As graduation approached, she cornered me one afternoon and said, with a steely expression etched across her face, "Priscilla, on your graduation day when you walk across that stage, your little nickname had better not be written anywhere on your diploma. Because no matter how many people call you that, it is *not* your name. I am the only person who has the right to give you your name. And I gave it to you the day you were born." Boom!

Do you see what she was saying? Other people didn't have the right to determine my name. Not even *I* had the right to give myself a name. Only the one who bore me was entitled to give me my name.

And that's what God has done for you.

Little sister, your Father gave you your name the moment you were born again. He called you righteous, royal, chosen, forgiven, free, and victorious. Your identity is forever wrapped up in who He calls you. No one else–not even you!–has the authority to give to you a label that doesn't align with your identity as His daughter. You are who *He* says you are. And like my mama's final word to me, God's Word is His final word to you on the way it's going to be. Got it? Got it.

Look at the first verse from Paul's letter to the Ephesians. He identifies the believers in this church by a name that God had given to them. What is it?

Was that a special name for the Ephesian Christians only? Look up a few more of Paul's opening words to some of the churches he wrote to. What does he call them in each of these verses?

> Paul, an apostle of Christ Jesus by God's will: To the faithful saints in Christ Jesus at Ephesus.
> *EPHESIANS 1:1*

1 Corinthians 1:2

2 Corinthians 1:1

Philippians 1:1

Colossians 1:2

"Saints." What are some of the images that come to mind when you picture someone with that title?

Historically, many faith traditions reserve the title of "saint" for certain people—usually dead people who did amazing enough things during their lifetimes that everybody now thinks of them as being somewhat of a spiritual superstar.

Paul, however, referred to *all* the believers as saints. To be a "saint" is another way of saying a person is "holy." (Isn't that one of the "who you are" statements you uncovered in Ephesians?) And believe it or not, God's been referring to all His people as "holy" for a long, long time.

"Now if you will carefully listen to me and keep my covenant, you will be my own possession out of all the peoples, although the whole earth is mine, and you will be my kingdom of priests and my holy nation."
EXODUS 19:5-6

To be "holy" means to be set apart, separated, consecrated, dedicated for a specific use or purpose.

Ancient Israel was known for centuries by the label "slaves." That's what everybody called them. It's what they called themselves. But God rescued them from slavery in Egypt and gave them a new name. A holy name. Do you see it there in Exodus 19:6 in the sidebar? "My holy nation."

Their new name was true of them no matter who they'd previously been. It was true of them no matter how they currently looked. It even took into account the many, *many* failings they were still going to commit in their future. But God chose them. He set them apart. And based on nothing other than the virtue of their relationship with Him, He declared them to be holy. They were *saints*. That's who the Israelites became when God brought them into covenant with Himself.

Let's see if He's done anything similar for you.

From what you know about the story of the ancient Israelites, what are some specific ways your life has been characterized at times by some of the same titles and descriptors?

Slaves:

Wanderers:

Rebels:

Idol worshipers:

Complainers:

Turn to 1 Peter 2:9-10. Write down each descriptor from this passage that God says is now true of you.

From the first moment I sat down at my computer to write this study, I've known the person I've been writing it for is a saint. Yeah, I've been talking today with a *saint*. *You!* That's your real name, your *given* name.

No matter what name you may mutter to yourself or have been called by someone else, you're a saint. No matter how you've lived up to the wrong kinds of names in your actions or attitudes, you're a saint. Think how many of those "who you are" identifications you wrote down at the beginning of this week are encapsulated in that fantastic label—*saint!* Your Father created you, found you, redeemed you, and called you. And He defines you as a saint.

It's time now to stop answering to any name that's out of character with who you really are. Don't live down to any other label. By God's Spirit, start living up to who you've been created to be in Him.

You, my little sister in Christ, are holy and set apart for the purposes of a holy God.

DOWN HERE, UP THERE

*He also raised us up with him and seated us
with him in the heavens in Christ Jesus.*
EPHESIANS 2:6

I HEARD ONCE about an older, English shopkeeper who made a good living by selling delicate, rich textiles and fabrics among the working class people of a small town in France. Not many of his customers were used to buying items of this quality, but he provided such excellent service and treated them with such personal care and kindness that they frequented his shop anyway.

Despite his considerable wealth, the man made it his daily habit to wear modest clothing, eat lunch with the locals at a humble bakery, and diligently learn the language and customs of the area so he could identify with the people he served. Then every evening after working hard all day, he'd flip the sign to "Closed," lock the door, turn off the lights, and go home.

He didn't need to go far.

At the back of his shop, a stone staircase led to a second story. Leaving behind his downstairs workplace, he'd remove the itchy cloak from around his shoulders and leave it on a hook, exposing a fine silk robe he'd worn underneath it all day. Then he'd step across the threshold into a luxurious apartment, his beautiful living quarters. All day long he lived below, but his real home was up above.

Blessed *be* the God and Father of our Lord Jesus Christ, who has blessed us with every spiritual blessing in the heavenly *places* in Chris,
EPHESIANS 1:3
(NASB)

Our lives as believers, to some extent, operate by this same principle. We live, work, play, and take part in all our activities with our feet firmly planted downstairs on the earth. But this world is not our home. Yes, the things we do here are important. They should be done well. They matter, as do all the people we do them with. But our real home, the place where we are ultimately rooted, find rest, and prepare for the next leg of our journey, is actually *upstairs*.

Sound a little too mystical? Let's bring it down to earth.

In the margin, draw a circle around the phrase that denotes our upstairs home. What does Paul say we're able to access there? And by how much?

Paul references this location several more times throughout the Book of Ephesians. Look up each of the following references and record all the important facts you discover about these "heavenly places." What's there? Who's there? What's happening there?

Ephesians 1:20-21

Ephesians 2:4-7

Ephesians 3:8-10

Ephesians 6:12

"Heavenly places."

I think you're going to like this place.

For one thing, Jesus is there. Did you notice that? In your analysis of Ephesians 1:20-21, did you note how God raised His Son from the dead and *seated* Him in heavenly places? That's important. Being seated was the symbolic posture of a king whose army had already been victorious in battle. Instead of standing, pacing, worrying himself to death, he could park himself on his throne as a visible statement of his complete and utter triumph.

But that's not even the best part, because *you* are seated there too, right (Eph. 2:6)? Not only does Jesus live in this invisible, unseen realm of total victory, but you've been given the right to live there in victory yourself. Turns out, you're not such an earthling after all. Sure, we see you walking around down here. But the place that dictates your real identity–the place that gives you your real purpose and perspective on life–is the place where you're seated with Christ. *Heavenly places.* Even as we speak, you're in both places at once.

Here's another way to look at it. I was recently on a video conference call with several people in a different state. They were all in Nashville, and I was in Dallas. Judging from my little picture that appeared along with theirs on the monitor, I was actively present with them in their office. They could see me. They could hear me. We could talk about the same things together. But I was really somewhere else. I was really at home in Texas (and will neither confirm nor deny that I was wearing my pajama pants).

Fully present on earth, and yet—through prayer, through worship, through communion with God—fully at home in heavenly places. That's where you are. That's *who* you are. The task now is for you to live with an *upstairs* perspective and perception while your feet are firmly planted *downstairs*.

Turn to Colossians 3 and read verses 1-3. What are the most practical ways you can "set your mind on things above" (v. 2)?

Read on to verses 5-9. From among this list of sinful behaviors, choose one that's a particular struggle for you. How would an upstairs mentality change your perspective and desire for participating in it?

Now read verses 12-15, a list of beautiful behaviors. What do you think are the main issues or pressures that keep believers from practicing these upstairs behaviors in their daily lives?

How does the theme of verse 17 display a heart that's living well in both places?

Heavenly place living is pretty sweet.

But not easy. Not a walk in the park. It requires intentionality, focus, and a consistent connection to the power source of the Holy Spirit. Did you also notice, in Ephesians 6:12, that the enemy and his demonic forces are in heavenly places, as well? Yeah, war is still raging there, with your opponent working like mad to discourage you from living in victory as a daughter of God. To be clear, it's a war he could never ultimately win, but if we aren't mindful, he can distract and discourage us so we don't get to experience our victory right now. Our adversary has already lost this war, but he fights just the same. Which is why, according to Ephesians 6, we have a required response to make.

According to Ephesians 6:13, what does Paul instruct us to do in order to avoid the enemy's schemes? Circle some of the action verbs that describe what your posture is supposed to be.

Never doubt your victory is assured, even in battle. Match the verses below with their descriptions of the devil's demise.

Philippians 2:9-11	All his works destroyed
Colossians 2:15	Destroyed, rendered powerless, broken
Hebrews 2:14	Will bow his knee to Jesus
1 John 3:8	Disarmed, disgraced, triumphed over

For this reason take up the full armor of God, so that you may be able to resist in the evil day, and having prepared everything, to take your stand.
EPHESIANS 6:13

Satan is fully aware that he cannot destroy you. It's much too late for that. The best he can do (and he intends to make full use of it) is to try making your time on earth futile and unproductive, to suffocate you with sin, insecurity, fear, and discouragement until you forget who you really are, until you forget where you truly reside. He can't "unseat" you, but he'll sure try to intimidate and paralyze you.

Good thing for you, though, you're in a position where you can show him who's boss. When you feel like you've had as much of him as you can stand, escape upstairs where you've always got a reserved seat and where the time is ticking on his doomsday clock.

VALUE STATEMENT

I pray that the eyes of your heart may be enlightened so that you may know what is the hope of his calling, what is the wealth of his glorious inheritance in the saints.
EPHESIANS 1:18

PICTURE THIS: You're sitting in the passenger seat of the car while your parent or a friend drives to a few stores on some Saturday afternoon errands. The two of you roll to a full stop at an intersection and wait for the light to change. In the few moments the car is stationary, you happen to look out the window and notice a dollar bill lying in the wide-open lane right next to you. Clearly someone dropped it by accident. The wind must have blown it there.

Rolling down the window for a closer look, you hear an audible gasp escape your lips. It's not a lost dollar; it's a hundred dollars. Quickly, you whip your head around to check for approaching traffic, while almost simultaneously grasping at the door latch and darting over to scoop up your find. *A hundred dollar bill!* You unfold it in your hands once you excitedly settle back into your seat. Obviously you'd give it back to its original owner if you could. But how could you ever find them?

The light turns green.

For the next few moments, you and the driver celebrate your good fortune. But as you look more closely, you discover the bill is not very pretty. It's been run over by quite a few cars. It's wearing visible tire marks. It's dirty and grimy. There's even a long rip straight down the center.

What would you do in this situation?

A. Throw the bill away because of its poor condition.

B. Circle back to the same place you found it and toss it in the road again, where it'll get more of the same treatment.

C. Cross out the amount on the bill, and write in a lesser value since it's become so dirty and torn.

D. Clean it off, tape the tear, and recognize it still bears intrinsic value no matter what it's been through.

I'm guessing D, right?

Of course. That money hasn't depreciated in value simply because it doesn't feel crisp and clean anymore, as if it just came from the bank.

Take a dollar bill of any amount from your purse or wallet. See how many items of documentation you can locate on its face that prove its authenticity. (Check all the ones you find.)

☐ signature

☐ official seal

☐ year printed

☐ stated dollar value

☐ unique serial number

☐ anything else? (watermark, city where bill was issued, etc.)

Why do each of these indicators carry greater importance than the bill's age or condition? What do they represent? What do they prove?

The intrinsic value of a piece of currency is ascribed by the government that issued it, not by what people do to it. And we as God's daughters don't lose our value either, merely because we've been through some incredibly difficult circumstances. Hardship, dysfunction, and sin do leave an impact, yes, but not on your *value.* Your worth and importance to His kingdom purpose remain unchanged.

What experiences from your life have sometimes made you feel as though they've lessened your value?

Turn to Ephesians 2:7-10. According to verse 7, your value as a saved sinner comes from how your brokenness puts what on display?

According to verse 8, who's responsible for you being a living exhibit of God's grace?

What percentage of anything you've done (or not done) has contributed to your standing with Him (v. 9)?

So according to verse 10, who are you?

For we are his workmanship, created in Christ Jesus for good works, which God prepared ahead of time for us to do. EPHESIANS 2:10

"I am God's workmanship." Be sure this statement appears in your list on page 86.

You are God's _____.

Your value is not in your good works. Your value is in the One who "prepared ahead of time" for you to do good works.

The Greek word for our English word "workmanship" is *poiema* (pronounced POY-ay-ma).[2] Originally it referred to a beautifully crafted work of art, whether a piece of architecture, poetry, sculpture, or something else. Like any meticulously fashioned specimen, its purpose is to show the mastery of the artist and leave an impression on the viewer.

This original word appears only one other time in Scripture, in a verse we actually studied back during our first week together. Romans 1:20 speaks of how God displayed His power and divine nature to humankind "through what he has made." *Poiema*. But listen to the way one pastor describes how God's "workmanship" of *you* is in a whole other class.

"The heavens and earth display the glory of God's material creation. But this is a new creation, called "saved sinners." They declare the glory of God's spiritual creation."[3]

And there is where your personal value lies.

In other words, your appearance is not the full extent of the "workmanship" God is interested in showing off. The realities of life may have left you feeling weak, depleted, and hopeless. For this reason, you may have begun considering your value diminished—perhaps not worthless, but *worth less*. Yet your true value assessment as a follower of Christ comes from letting the fruit of your new heart overflow so others can see the life-changing power of God's grace inside you. This is what all masterpieces do. They inspire and enlighten others. You, as one of God's masterpieces, make others believe they can change because you have been changed. Your life as God's *poiema* whets their appetite to know the masterful Artist who personally fashioned you from a "piece of work" to a "work of art."

That's what Paul prayed the Ephesian believers would see—that their value was in *who they were*, in what God had already made them to be.

Turn to Ephesians 1 and answer the following questions beginning with verse 15.

What did Paul "never stop giving thanks for" when he thought about them? What did he love hearing most about them (v. 15-16)?

What did he know that only the Holy Spirit could give them, whenever they had doubts about their intrinsic worth (v. 17)?

What three things do these two verses identify as the sources of a believer's value? What did Paul say he wanted the Ephesians to know about Christ (v. 18-19)?

The hope of his _____.

The wealth of his glorious _____ in the saints.

The immeasurable greatness of his _____ toward us who believe.

In closing, use Ephesians 1:18-19 to create your own prayer to the Lord. Ask Him to open up your heart to understand the value of *who you are*, and to enable you to think and behave from this perspective of worth despite what may have happened in your life.

You are already worth so much more than you know.

WEEK 4 · DAY 5
HALF DAY

THIS WEEK we've had the opportunity to look closely at *who you are* as a daughter of God. Everything in your life changes–your perspectives, your attitudes, your ambitions, your thought patterns, everything–when you begin to grasp your identity in Him.

We've learned a lot, haven't we? We sure have.

So on our half day this go-round, I'd like you to step back and process things a little bit. Flip to page 86, where you began compiling your list of "who you are" statements from your reading of Ephesians 1–2 at the beginning of the week. Hopefully you've been able to add a few more to the list as we've probed more deeply into those chapters.

Read through your list again, and choose three of these biblical truths that have proven the most memorable to you. Using the blank journaling lines below, spend a little time writing about why you think they've struck you with such force.

Be sure to include at least one of the specific Bible verses that backs up this claim of "who you are."

1. "I am _____."

_____

_____

_____

2. "I am _____."

_____

_____

_____

3. "I am _____."

_____

_____

_____

I'm delighted you've picked up so much biblical information about your identity, your position in heavenly places, and how you can align your life with who you truly are in Christ.

Finally, I'd like you to do just one more little exercise, for old times' sake. Do you remember in one of our first interactions, way back on page 12, when I originally asked you the question, "Who are you?" I wonder if you recall some of the things you wrote down then.

Today, having been through four weeks of learning what God says about your identity—and especially having been through this week, where we've focused on the "who you are" question even more directly—how would you reword your identity now?

Take a quick stab at describing that.

Good job this week. So much growth and progress! And I've got a feeling next week will be even more impactful in your life and spiritual journey. See you soon.

Week Five

WHAT YOU HAVE

PRESS PLAY

Use the space below to follow along and take any notes as you watch the video for Week 5.

When you know what your _____ is, you can stop living _____ your spiritual means.

You have full disposal of the King of Kings and the Lord of Lords _____ to you.

[He] has blessed us with every _____ _____ (Eph. 1:3, NASB).

He has _____ given it to you.

Who is someone you know that is facing something very difficult but is living with the peace and joy of Christ?

You already have _____ that you need to carry you through it.

The Holy Spirit is the _____ person of the _____.

LET'S TALK

I **PLAYED** a little basketball in my time, though not enough to advance to collegiate level. Only now as my gigantic sons have taken up competitive sports have I really grown in my understanding and appreciation of the game.

Now to the untrained eye, the only thing a basketball player is interested in doing is scoring a goal, sinking the shot. Everybody seems to be out there basically doing the same thing—running around, wanting the ball. But that's not altogether true. One player may be coming out to the foul line to set a pick (a block), trying to separate one of his teammates from a defender. Another player may be looking to pass to an open man cutting to the basket. Another may actually be moving *away* from the goal, clearing out room in the lane for everybody else, while someone else is positioning for a rebound if a shot fails to go in and bounces off.

What I'm saying is—if you only just showed up and didn't know what you were watching for, all you'd see is basically one big tangle of uncoordinated activity. But once you better understand what's happening out there, you pick up more on the essential roles and varied expertise that help the whole *team* score a basket.

Last week, I asked you to read the first two chapters of Ephesians. Maybe it's the first time you'd ever done that. Up until then, perhaps all you knew of Ephesians 1–2 were a couple of underlined memory verses, if that. Now, though, you've sat through the whole game. You've watched every play. You've seen how a lot of the pieces fit together. In particular, you've come away with a sizable number of "who you are" statements about your Christian identity that have been sitting there in your Bible *all this time*. Now, they're here in your book and, best of all, tucked away inside your heart.

You're not just a rookie spectator anymore.

> **Looking back at the statements from Week 4, which one did God remind you of this week?**

> **How did knowing these statements affect your thoughts or actions? Did they change the way you see yourself or your response to a circumstance you faced?**

So this week, since you've already done so well at seeing the big picture, I want you to have an opportunity to dig deeper and discover the numerous layers of insight in the text. One of my favorite Bible study techniques is the *slow* read. This is where you only commit to a few verses at a time, and you don't just read them as quickly as you can. *Okay, I'm finished.* No, you savor them. You mull over them. You focus in on one word or phrase. Then you close your eyes and swish that single verse around in your head for a few minutes, asking God to show you anything else you didn't notice at first… something that makes it matter at this moment, on this day, in your life. See what I'm saying?

Here is my plan for you today—actually for every day this week. I've broken down Ephesians 1–2 into six shorter portions. And each day, when you open your book to do your study this week, I want you to start by coming back to this section *first* and reading the selection of verses assigned to that day.

Underneath each day's passage are some journaling lines, like last week. Only this time, I want you looking for something different from what you gathered last week. With your foundation of "who you are" declarations already in place, I want you to search for "what you have" as a believer in Christ.

For example, in Ephesians 1:3, Paul says we've been "blessed."

> Blessed is the God and Father of our Lord
> Jesus Christ, who has blessed us with every
> spiritual blessing in the heavens in Christ,
> **EPHESIANS 1:3**

Based on that verse, fill in the blanks below:

I have _____ spiritual _____.

Maybe one of the identity statements you included in your list last week was "I am blessed." And, of course, you are! It's fantastic. You are blessed. What a great thing to know! But if I was reading this same verse from the perspective of wanting to learn what I *have*, I could also say, "I *have* every spiritual blessing in the heavens in Christ."

Do you see how this tells you even more? More than "I am blessed" does? It shines a light on what Paul says is your "inheritance" (Eph. 1:11,14,18) as a follower of Jesus. It's another way of measuring your identity, of adding to what your identity in Christ includes. Your identity in Him is not just one thing; it's a whole bunch of stuff. And I want you knowing about all the stuff He's given you to carry around.

So let's start here today and do the first eight verses of Ephesians 1 together. You'll see I've left you room to make notes on what God reveals to you as you read. If you need more room, just go grab a piece of paper or a journal. When you finish going through today's portion (Eph. 1:1-8), skip to the next page and let me tell you goodbye before you go off into the rest of your week.

Today: Ephesians 1:1-8

I have _____

_____

_____

Day 1: Ephesians 1:9-14

I have _____

_____

_____

Day 2: Ephesians 1:15-23

I have _____

_____

_____

Day 3: Ephesians 2:1-5

I have _____

_____

_____

Day 4: Ephesians 2:6-13

I have _____

_____

_____

Day 5: Ephesians 2:14-22

I have _____

_____

_____

Two things I'd like to leave with you:

Each of these Bible study tools I've been showing you is just another way to read and learn from the Scriptures throughout your life. Even when you don't have a devotional book or study guide for help, you can always just pick up your Bible, start reading and writing, and God's Spirit will spark life into it every time.

Second, and finally, the "I have" statements you're starting to compile are building up what I'd like to call your *Inheritance Benefits Package*. They're your personal catalog of spiritual perks that God lavishly pours out on all His kids. I'll use this term again throughout our week of study—Inheritance Benefits Package—and when you see it, you'll know what I'm talking about: all these blessings you're writing down on this page. Remember to swing back here at the beginning of every day this week to add more.

Ready to get a load of all the things God has given you and keeps giving you and will never stop giving you?

Me too!

Let's go!

WINDFALL

In him we have also received an inheritance.
EPHESIANS 1:11

AN AFRICAN SAFARI is spectacular for about a million reasons, most of which come from seeing these incredible animals in real life. There's no way to single out any one of them as being my favorite. But today for some reason—as I sit here thinking about the safari we took a few years ago with our boys, about two hours out of Cape Town—I'm remembering the African impala.

Impalas are these sleek, sinewy, amazingly fast antelopes, best known for their ability to jump to astounding heights. In one mighty leap, they can spring ten feet off the ground and cover more than thirty feet in distance. Which is why maybe the most remarkable piece of information we learned about the impala is that in captivity, all it takes to keep them contained is a three-foot-high fence. Even though they could clear that puny level of enclosure in what would amount to a bunny hop, the obstructed visibility hinders their potential, and here's why: impalas will not jump into a space they cannot see.

This week, dear sister, I want to help you begin to deconstruct the puny fences the enemy has set up to keep you from jumping headlong into abundant life. I want to expand your field of spiritual vision. I want to make it as wide as that South African vista where we saw the impalas with their curly antlers and all their free-range possibilities. I want you to see—*really* see—the depths of God's love in choosing you, adopting you, bestowing grace upon you, and redeeming you, so you can jump into the victorious life with both feet. Never lose sight of it, because if you do, you'll live your life feeling limited by narrow, rigid lies and deceptions that are well below what you've been created to experience.

Did you remember to start your study today back on page 110, reading Ephesians 1:9-14? In case you forgot, take a moment to do that now. If one of the things you wrote in your book was "I have an inheritance," (v. 11) that's good, because that's what we're talking about today. What are some benefits that go along with having an inheritance?

Here's some backstory on the folks to whom Paul wrote Ephesians. These Christians occasionally felt like second-class citizens. They loved Jesus, they loved each other, and they loved what their new faith was changing in their hearts. But they were Gentiles. They were outsiders. (Ever felt that way? I have.) In their estimation, the Jews—the physical descendants of Abraham—would always be the ones who claimed the closest connection to the God of the Bible.

Paul had been born a Jew. At one time he'd strictly held to the spiritual superiority of his natural race. But God had given him insight into a "mystery," something that had not been "known to people in other generations as it is now revealed to his holy apostles and prophets by the Spirit" (Eph. 3:4-5).

The Gentiles, he said, were insiders too.

> The Gentiles are coheirs, members of the same body, and partners in the promise in Christ Jesus through the gospel.
> *EPHESIANS 3:6*

> **Look at Ephesians 3:6 in your margin. What identifier does Paul give to Gentiles?**
> A. Cohorts   C. Co-champs
> B. Co-owners   D. Coheirs

> **Turn to Galatians 3:29 in your Bible. What else does Paul say a Gentile believer in Christ has been given the right to claim?**

Here's what Paul was telling them. The reach of God's blessing, through Jesus, now extended beyond Abraham's offspring—his descendants, his children, his seed—and had come to include (gasp!) people who were not of Jewish descent. The Ephesians were now "members of the same body." By means of the gospel, God had brought them together with all those who professed Jesus as Lord (along with you and me now)—people from every race, culture, and background, united into one family. As heirs. *Coheirs.*

> **This "mystery," by the way, is something God really enjoys bragging about. Turn to Ephesians 3:8-9 and tell me how long He'd been holding this news in before Jesus came and changed everything?**

> **Now look at Ephesians 3:10-11. Who does God want to tell about these riches He's decided to pour out on people of every make and model all over the world?**

I'm sorry, I'm having a difficult time holding in my own joy as well, thinking about the riches that are now yours and mine because of Jesus' sacrifice for us on the cross. But I've got to tell you, it gets even better. Not only are we coheirs with *one another*, look at this:

The Spirit himself testifies together with our spirit that we are God's children, and if children, also heirs— heirs of God and coheirs with Christ
ROMANS 8:16-17

Read the verses from Romans 8 in the margin. We are "coheirs" with who?

What would you guess to be the quality and quantity of your inheritance, knowing that God Himself is your Father and benefactor, and that Jesus is your brother and fellow heir?

As I mentioned before, when Paul used the word "heir" in reference to our standing with the Father, he was reaching back into the long history of God's people when the Lord had promised Abraham, Isaac, and Jacob that their descendants would take possession of the land that God had promised to give them. Moses, in repeating these promises to the Lord one day, said:

> "Remember your servants Abraham, Isaac, and Israel— you swore to them by yourself and declared, 'I will make your offspring as numerous as the stars of the sky and will give your offspring all this land that I have promised, and they will inherit it forever.'"
> *EXODUS 32:13*

Forever. The term describing this inheritance carries the idea of being a *permanent* and *assured* possession.

Fill in the blanks using the italicized words above.

For ancient Israel, being an heir meant they had _____ and _____ possession of everything God had given them.

And since you, too, are a part of this family of God, you can say it as well: For me, being an heir of God means I have _____ and _____ possession of everything God has given me.

Of course, there's a whole lot more available now than just a plot of land in the Middle East to claim as your inheritance. You have "every spiritual blessing in the heavens in Christ" (Eph. 1:3), remember? Permanently and assuredly yours. Nothing can separate them from you because God has declared you an heir.

Whether or not you *experience* them? That's up to you. But whether or not they've been placed at your disposal? That's an unchanging fact. You have full access to every single drop of goodness and abundance that God wants to give you as His daughter. His heir.

It's yours.

Get it in your eyesight and then step up—*leap up*—into the inheritance your Father has given you.

TWIN BLESSINGS

*Grace to you and peace from God our
Father and the Lord Jesus Christ.*
EPHESIANS 1:2

PAUL WROTE thirteen letters that appear in our New Testament. That's almost half the total number of books, and in that time, he taught on many different spiritual insights that continue to encourage, caution, and challenge Christians to become everything God has redeemed them through Christ to be. But if you'll notice, at the beginning of every letter he included the exact same statement, often word for word. He opened each writing with a nearly identical compound blessing.

Here's the entire collection (minus only Ephesians 1:2, which already appears at the top of this page).

- Romans 1:7
- 1 Corinthians 1:3
- 2 Corinthians 1:2
- Galatians 1:3
- Philippians 1:2
- Colossians 1:2
- 1 Thessalonians 1:1
- 2 Thessalonians 1:2
- 1 Timothy 1:2
- 2 Timothy 1:2
- Titus 1:4
- Philemon 1:3

Check out two or three of these. What are the twin blessings that Paul highlights as being part of everyone's spiritual inheritance who believes in Jesus Christ?

_____ **and** _____

The only problem with words like these–*grace* and *peace*–is that by their frequent use, we recognize them as sounding significant without always understanding what they mean. But we need to know what God has given us in these two blessings. They are, after all, part of our inheritance.

Let's start with *grace*.

Grace is undeserved favor and acceptance. Grace is what we need from God to save us, because there's no way we can ever earn His approval otherwise. By His undeserved kindness–just because He has chosen to love us–He has decided that what Jesus did on the cross is suitable payment for the cost of our sins. Even though we still deserve to die for what we've done, He accepts Christ's righteous blood in place of ours.

But grace doesn't just save us; it also sustains us. We live under an umbrella of God's favor every single day. His grace keeps us going. Again, though He owes us nothing, He chooses by His grace to support us, honor us, care for us, and provide for us, to extend continuous kindness to us—not only to save our souls for eternity but also to make it possible for us to live freely and fully, without guilt, shame, or fear, right now.

That's *grace*—or at least a little bit of it.

> **Underline the portions from the last couple of paragraphs that are most helpful to you in understanding grace.**
>
> **If you were teaching a fifth-grade Sunday school class, how would you define grace to them in simple terms, using some of the insights I just gave you? Write your response below.**

The original Greek word translated "grace" is *charis* (pronounced KHAH-res).[1] The hard *k* sound at the front is actually a little gargly, sort of like you're trying to clear something from the back of your throat. (Try it. It's fun.)

When Paul said "grace to you" to each person reading his letter, the reason he could say it was because he'd received it. In 2 Corinthians 12, for example, he'd been having a real problem. We don't know the exact nature of it (Paul didn't say), but it was so overwhelmingly frustrating to him that he'd prayed fervently about it, asking God more than once to *please* take it away.

> **In my life, I've had problems that I've felt that upset about. Have you? What were they?**

> **Look up 2 Corinthians 12:9. Instead of taking away Paul's problem, what did God give him?**

> **What did He say Paul needed to feel inside in order to see God's strength in action?**

> **How did Paul change his own attitude and perspective on his circumstances?**

Like Paul, I know you deal with problems that you sometimes don't know how you can survive. (You just shared one of them with me.) And many times, even though you beg God to remove it, He doesn't.

But *grace*. He gives grace. He supports and sustains you. He carries you through. He bestows upon you a part of your inheritance that allows you to experience Him in ways that (sometimes) are even sweeter and stronger than if He'd taken away your whole problem. Amazingly, you find you can learn to *rejoice*, like Paul, for the weaknesses you feel, because they lead you into a deeper encounter with the bountiful grace of God.

How have you already seen and felt God's sustaining grace, in the context of some of your most difficult life experiences?

And then there's *peace*.

"I have grace."
"I have peace."
In the logs you've been keeping on page 110 this week, did you include these two spiritual blessings? Have you completed the verses for Day 2? If not, don't forget to do that before we close today.

I've heard a commentator connect the two this way: "*Grace* is the fountain. *Peace* belongs to the stream of spiritual blessings which issues from this fountain."[2] The peace of God is the smile of God that soothes your soul on the inside, even when your circumstances are difficult on the outside. It's an internal calm that no external factors can alter.

How might you define the relationship between grace and peace in your own words?

"Peace I leave with you. My peace I give to you. I do not give to you as the world gives. Don't let your heart be troubled or fearful."
JOHN 14:27

In the days and hours before Jesus went to the cross, His closest friends (His disciples) were understandably distraught. But He comforted them by telling them He would not be leaving them without guidance or direction after He was gone. He promised them *peace*–a permanent, restful assurance that no obstacle or opposition could diminish or destroy. His peace would be like an inner sense of settledness that no enemy could touch because it rested deep within their hearts, locked inside their souls.

Even after Jesus presented Himself alive to His disciples following His resurrection, what were His first words to them? (See John 20:19.)

Read on to verses 20-21. What did He say again?

Why did He know they'd still need peace, even though they were happy and relieved in the moment?

While you're there, why don't you go ahead and read verse 22, where Jesus gives them the gift of peace Himself in the person of His Holy Spirit. God's unshakable, internal peace would now be their constant companion. (We'll be talking more about the Holy Spirit real soon.)

Think of someone you know who demonstrates what it means to live in peace despite difficult circumstances. Have they ever said anything to you about how they're able to live that way?

What difference does it make to you, knowing that "peace from God" is not only a possibility for you but is actually a guaranteed part of your Inheritance Benefits Package?

Your heavenly Father has committed to you His grace and peace as valuable elements of your spiritual inheritance. What a tragedy not to access and take full advantage of what you've been given. Your spiritual bank account is always open, and you can make instant, constant withdrawals.

Don't worry about anything, but in everything, through prayer
and petition with thanksgiving, present your requests to God.
And the peace of God, which surpasses all understanding,
will guard your hearts and minds in Christ Jesus.
PHILIPPIANS 4:6-7 (EMPHASIS MINE)

Look at the highlighted word in Philippians 4:6-7. This is the key that unlocks the peace of God in your life. End today by crafting a prayer to God. Present your requests, of course, but sprinkle in a heavy dose of gratitude for all the things He's already done. See if you don't gradually notice His peace growing within you.

INHERITANCE IN WRITING

*In him we have redemption through his blood, the forgiveness
of our trespasses, according to the riches of his grace*
EPHESIANS 1:7

I REMEMBER sitting with my husband in our lawyer's office drafting our will and being given some of the most difficult questions and scenarios I've ever thought about. My husband and I felt a bit overwhelmed by all we had to decide. Chief among our concerns were issues related to our children in the event we were no longer around to care for them. We thought through all our worldly assets, determining how we'd want them allotted to the boys for their use and blessing. It led to some intense, highly detailed conversations.

But one matter was easy and undisputed. We were completely unified in knowing *our* children would be the recipients of our inheritance. Jackson, Jerry Jr., and Jude are without doubt the three beneficiaries written down in our will.

What does our desire to leave them an inheritance tell you about our...
- **relationship with them?**

- **feelings toward them?**

- **concern for their future?**

In the family of God, the mere fact that you're an heir means you're the child of a heavenly Father who loves you deeply and wants you to experience the benefits of His provision for you. Obviously, your inheritance in Christ has an eternal value that reaches far beyond your life here on earth. But God has carefully considered the resources you need *now*, as well. He wants you equipped to navigate the here and now with the things He's already given you.

In today's section of reading on page 110—Ephesians 2:1-5—you looked again at the salvation God has brought to your life. What was something new you noticed in that short passage that maybe you hadn't seen when reading it before?

The two items from your Inheritance Benefits Package that I'd like to unpack with you today are related to what you read there.

How are "redemption" and "forgiveness" tied together (Eph. 1:7)?

Why are they only available "in him"?

All throughout the Old Testament and into the New, the term *redemption* referred to someone offering payment or ransom to buy something back. It meant a price had been paid and an action had been taken to change ownership. For example, it's why God could say to the Israelites in Egypt, "I will redeem you with an outstretched arm and great acts of judgment" (Ex. 6:6). They once belonged to their slave owners, but now God was buying them back for Himself. They could walk in freedom and victory because they had been *redeemed*.

The same is true for you. Look at this:

What is the major contrasting idea expressed in the two verses to the right?

In your experience, what does it look like when a person is a "slave of sin"?

What about someone who's been released and set free from their sins?

How does the enemy use feelings of guilt to try counteracting what Jesus' blood has done to redeem you?

What would living free from even the *guilt* of sin look and feel like?

Jesus responded, "Truly I tell you, everyone who commits sin is a slave of sin."
JOHN 8:34

[Jesus] loves us and has set us free from our sins by his blood,
REVELATION 1:5

When I was in college at the University of Houston, the Lord seared a Bible verse into my heart (Gal. 5:1) that has been a compass for me ever since. I'd say it's become my life verse—a constant reminder of the kind of life I'm redeemed to live.

Look up Galatians 5:1 in your Bible, and write it in your own words below.

What a pity for a freed person to continue living *by choice* like a slave. Not only does it take away from the fact that Jesus paid the price to free them, but it reveals the needless torment of staying shackled to a chain from which you've already been released.

You don't need to live that way! You've been purchased from sin. This is redemption. God has stripped sin of the right and power to boss you around, to tell you what to do. It can't require you to sacrifice your dignity in small increments of compromise and lapses in integrity. Stand firm in your freedom every single day of your life and enjoy the abundant life He's granted to you by virtue of your inheritance.

Remembering your *redemption* and living in the light of it can change your entire life!

And along with redemption comes *forgiveness.*

Underline the key words or phrases in each of the following verses. Which one ministers the most to you?

> As far as the east is from the west, so far has he removed our transgressions from us.
> **PSALM 103:12**

> "I have wiped out your transgressions like a thick cloud and your sins like a heavy mist."
> **ISAIAH 44:22 (NASB)**

> "For I will forgive their iniquity and never again remember their sin."
> **JEREMIAH 31:34**

Each verse points out the full removal of your sin. Out of sight; out of mind. Not only does God remove your sins from His view, but He also chooses not to recall them ever again. He could, of course. (He knows everything.) But He doesn't. He chooses not to. He's made up His mind not to remember them.

That's how *forgiven* you are.

You have absolute pardon from your sins.

Sound good? Sounds *great*.

It means you can come to Him in boldness without ever worrying that He's mad at you or that He's unwilling to hear you and respond to you. It also means whenever negative circumstances crop up in your life, you don't need to wonder if He's punishing you for something you've done. Sure, He may be *disciplining* you because He loves you, better than any good parent could. You may also be enduring the natural consequences that result from sinful actions. That's part of His loving discipline, as well. But God doesn't have unguarded bouts of anger that make Him have knee-jerk reactions of frustration toward you. Listen, God is *not mad* at you. No matter what you've done. He's erased the memory of your sin.

You are *forgiven*!

Tell me about the sigh of relief you feel from truly believing what I just told you.

The only thing I'd add, as you consider the immensity of these gifts from God, is not to waste your inheritance–His *redemption* and His *forgiveness*. For with inheritance comes responsibility. A bountiful inheritance, properly received, is the kind that can lead to significant changes in the way you live.

How does your treatment toward those who've sinned against you compare with God's treatment of you and your sin against Him? Are you equally quick to forgive, extend grace, and resist being offended? Why or why not?

Write down the names of any people in your life that you should forgive, just as He has forgiven you. Ask the Lord to empower you to offer it to them today.

UNDERNEATH IT ALL

> Now we have this treasure in clay jars, so that this
> extraordinary power may be from God and not from us.
> *2 CORINTHIANS 4:7*

I'M NOT into trashing people for the choices they make in life, but we've got some friends who've literally trashed just about everything around them. The garbage dump they own is the largest waste management business in the entire southwestern region of the United States.

As you can imagine, they hear their share of jokes. Thankfully they can easily laugh them off, comforted in knowing they own *2,000 acres* where people's trash is safely collected, eliminated, and properly recycled every day. Maybe even some of your own if you live in the southeast part of America.

Actually, though, that's not the only reason their faces break into broad smiles when they think about this enormous piece of property that's made them so successful in business. Several years ago, engineers with the state government discovered a fresh underground spring located deep underneath their land. The source is so massive that, if needed, it could supply a huge portion of Texas with all its water for decades.

Other people may look at these friends and see only the fun-loving couple who runs the garbage dump. But in actuality, they are so much more. Underneath all that trash, they have a natural treasure.

In Him, you also, after listening to the message of truth, the gospel of your salvation— having also believed, you were sealed in Him with the Holy Spirit of promise, *EPHESIANS 1:13 (NASB)*

Before we move any further along in our study today, take some time to finish your "I have" statements on page 110, if you haven't already. Then look at Ephesians 1:13 in the margin and answer the following questions:

What is the treasure you received as part of your inheritance?

When did you receive this gift?

What is He called in this verse? "the Holy Spirit of _____"

The Holy Spirit. Of all the unbelievable blessings that comprise your Inheritance Benefits Package, the greatest gift you'll ever receive on this side of eternity is something–Someone– who took up residence in you the moment you placed faith in Jesus.

> **The Holy Spirit has actually been here all along. Turn to the first two verses of the Bible—Genesis 1:1-2—and tell me where you see Him.**

> **When was He there? While what was happening?**

> **What was He doing?**

> **What are some key insights you can draw about the Holy Spirit from the observations you made in this passage?**

I know it's a little difficult to understand–a *lot* difficult to understand–but God is actually a unity of three unique persons (Father, Son, and Spirit) who come together into what we call the Trinity. He is not three separate gods; He is *one* God. But again, it's infinitely more complicated than our finite minds are capable of grasping. And yet all three were present at creation.

> **Look down to Genesis 1:26. What kind of pronouns does the Bible use when it describes the first human being made in the image of God?**

"Let *us* make man in *our* image," right? The Holy Spirit was involved in that.

So when we think of the Spirit of God who comes to live in us at salvation, we're not talking about a lesser, watered-down, weakened version of Himself. The same God who was there at the beginning, creating the entire universe, now lives inside of you. Pretty powerful, wouldn't you say? And multitalented, let me tell you …

Here's a small, biblical sampling of the benefits God's Spirit brings to your life. Draw a line to connect the Scripture verse with the attribute or function it describes.

John 14:16	He prays for me, and He intercedes for me.
John 16:8	He produces godly character in me.
Romans 8:26	He convicts me about my sin.
1 Corinthians 2:10	He sanctifies me, purifies me.
1 Corinthians 12:4-5	He strengthens me on the inside.
2 Corinthians 3:5-6	He helps me; He counsels me.
Galatians 5:22-23	He gives me gifts to use in serving Him.
Ephesians 3:16	He reveals the mind of God to me.
2 Thessalonians 2:13	He takes me beyond my natural ability.

Circle at least two of the actions from this list that you most frequently see Him doing in your life.

How has He worked through one of these qualities to impact a choice you made or a direction you decided to take?

How do you behave differently because of what the Holy Spirit does inside you?

How do you think differently?

How do you feel differently?

How does His influence impact the way you react to difficult people or situations?

I wish I had more time, although honestly there's never enough time to contemplate the total makeover the Holy Spirit is able to accomplish in us when we just say, "Hey, why don't *You* take charge here and change me into somebody new." *God Himself* lives inside you. If that ever grows uninteresting to you, you're paying far too much attention to far lesser things.

> The Holy Spirit is the down payment of our inheritance, until the redemption of the possession, to the praise of his glory.
> *EPHESIANS 1:14*

To understand a little more about the Holy Spirit's nature and how He factors into your inheritance, consider the verse in the margin from Ephesians 1:14.

"The Holy Spirit is the _____ _____ of our _____."

If you looked up this same verse in your own Bible, the word "down payment" might be translated instead as a deposit, a pledge, a guarantee, an installment. It's like when you're making a major purchase, and they'll sometimes allow you to pay only a portion of the asking price as a promise that you'll be paying off the rest of the balance at a later time.

I mean, it's pretty incredible what the Holy Spirit is charged to do for you right now, already. The things He makes happen in you can turn you into a whole new person—somebody who lives differently, talks differently, eats differently, relates differently. He enables you to live on the earth as heir to a spiritual fortune. But the part you get to experience today is only a small percentage of the huge windfall that's coming to you—*promised* to you—on the other side of eternity. The part you can't entirely know today is how great it's going to be. The part you can absolutely know right now is that it's guaranteed to be.

No matter what life throws at you, little sis, you never need to worry that God won't be big enough to handle it with you. He will make good on every single promise He's made. You not only have an inheritance; you have the Giver of the inheritance making Himself at home right there in your living space. You could not be more equipped, more protected, or more empowered than you're currently able to be at every moment.

I have the Holy Spirit of promise.

That's the best news either one of us has heard all day.

End today's lesson by writing out a prayer of thanks for the remarkable promise God is actively working in you, knowing that "he who started a good work in you will carry it on to completion until the day of Christ Jesus" (Phil. 1:6).

I'M PRETTY EXCITED HERE. I've been reading through Ephesians 1–2 with you this week, a little bit at a time, and while I know I'm a grown adult, I don't ever want to outgrow being energized by what I've been reading. "What we have" is amazing, agreed? Our inheritance is incredible.

You have done amazing work all week finding your "I have" statements, so now I want you to take time to finish up with Ephesians 2:14-22 before moving on.

Go ahead.

I'll wait.

Pick out your favorite two or three statements you found in Ephesians 1–2, and write down what excites you the most about them. Just like on this day last week, write down the verse reference where you found each of these truths. In case you ever forget, I want you to know how to get back there and be reminded of it all over again.

1. "I have _____."

_____

_____

_____

_____

_____

2. "I have _____."

_____

_____

_____

_____

_____

3. "I have_____."

_____

_____

_____

_____

I suggest we close our week with a final observation. When I was studying Ephesians 1 this week, I came across a fascinating perspective on verse 11, where Paul talks about how we've "received an inheritance." One of the commentaries I was studying said this phrase could be translated, "we were claimed by God as his portion."[3]

In other words, not only has God given us an inheritance in Him, but also He deems us so valuable and worth His while that He claims us as His own inheritance, too! He loves us that much.

Turn to Deuteronomy 32:9. How does Moses describe the people of Israel?

How might this same idea hold true for us, who've been adopted into the people of God and included with Abraham's offspring? (Remember 1 Peter 2:9—"You are a chosen race, a royal priesthood, a holy nation, a people for his possession … ")

How does this concept make you feel about the importance God places on your identity?

We've learned a lot about "who we are." We've learned a lot about "what we have." To see a more comprehensive list of our blessings and benefits in Christ that are scattered throughout the Bible, turn to page 191. The only thing that could possibly be better would be learning what it takes to let these things change "how we live."

I'd love to talk with you more about that. And we will, next week.

See you then.

Week Six

WALK
THIS WAY

PRESS PLAY

Use the space below to follow
along and take any notes as you
watch the video for Week 6.

Walking requires _____.

Walk by the _____ of _____.

What does it look like for you to be a woman who walks differently?

We live in a world where you are going to have to _____ what kind of _____ you are going to be.

Postchristianity is the loss of the primacy of the _____ worldview.[1]

How are your friends and the people around you helping or hurting your ability to walk well as a follower of Christ?

Walk in a manner that is _____ of the _____ that is on your life.

I **ENJOY** an occasional run. In fact, I like to think of myself as a runner, although I don't know if that's what anyone else would call it when I'm out there in my sweats and sneakers, struggling through a few miles of track. It's not easy, but that's sort of the point. Running is intended to push you and demand something from you. It's supposed to be a panting, foot-pounding test of endurance. Running makes you sweat. Running gives your lungs a workout. It's not meant to be the normal method of transportation you take around the house or at school or every time you need to go somewhere.

That's what walking is for, right? Walking is the true cadence of life. And in the Bible, when God wants to communicate what He expects you to do with all the things He's done for you, His main instruction is simply to start walking.

> **Look up the following verses on what it means to "walk" out your life as a Christ follower and read each one aloud. Match them to the correlating instruction.**
>
> | | |
> |---|---|
> | **Romans 13:13** | **Walk the same way Jesus walked.** |
> | **Galatians 5:16** | **Walk worthy of the Lord, pleasing to Him.** |
> | **Ephesians 5:1-2** | **Walk how the Spirit wants, not how your flesh wants.** |
> | **Colossians 1:10** | **Walk as you'd want to be seen if walking in broad daylight.** |
> | **1 John 2:6** | **Walk in love, because you've been dearly loved.** |

The Bible does sometimes refer to life as being a race we run. "Run in such a way to win the prize" (1 Cor. 9:24). "Let us run with endurance the race that lies before us" (Heb. 12:1). When looking at life from the long view, when you see the whole thing at once, life is indeed a marathon. It's a long-distance race.

But from a practical standpoint, we experience life as a daily walk. From the basis of how we approach life every day, it's primarily a one-foot-in-front-of-the-other routine. Often when we're told to run in the Bible, it's to run away from temptation. "Flee sexual immorality," the Bible says (1 Cor. 6:18). "Flee from these things, and pursue righteousness, godliness, faith, love," and so on (1 Tim. 6:11).

Other than that, we start the day, and we start walking—moving forward and progressing in our life of faith. And whether you realize it or not, that's exactly what you've been working on throughout this entire study. You've been practicing your walking skills. You've been training yourself to be intentional about the steps you're choosing to take.

How worn were your spiritual walking shoes before we started this study? Were you moving forward in your relationship with the Lord?

How has your pace changed in the last six weeks?

Have you ever been sidetracked from your walk with God? What got you off track, and how were you able to get back in stride with Him?

Being intentional about how we walk is half the battle. In our physical lives, walking is such a common activity for most of us that we rarely think about it while we're doing it. But in our spiritual lives, we can't afford to be so passive. Instead, we need to watch where we're going, looking to be sure we're not stepping into enemy fire, that each step is planted on something firm, and that we're headed toward our intended destination.

So, yes, you've been putting new stuff into your head and your heart while we've been doing this study together. But that's not all. Every bit of it has come with application for your feet.

Your identity is a *walking* identity.

Let me show you what I mean. For the past couple of weeks, you've been letting Scripture educate you on "who you are" and "what you have" as a follower of Jesus. This is your in-Christ identity. Along the way, you've also written insights on some of the most memorable elements of your identity.

In the chart on the following page, list several of your favorite identity statements in the left-hand portion of the grid. Then in the blank space on the right, adapt that statement into a "walking instruction." Tell me how the truth of your identity translates into a change in your walking style.

Your Identity	What It Walks Like

If you're having a difficult time figuring out what to put here, let me see if I can help.

One of the first identity statements we wrote down was "I am chosen." This makes me think of one of my dear friends who's experienced a lifetime, really, of rejection by those who should have loved her most. She went through her entire childhood without ever knowing her father because he abandoned her and her mother at an early age. Then as an adult, her fiancé called off the wedding they'd begun planning following their official engagement. How excruciating the pain from these two significant periods of her life. She often grappled with an intense feeling of abandonment. But those sweet words of Christ–"You did not choose me, but I chose you" (John 15:16)–have been like healing balms of love and grace poured into her soul.

She walks differently today, because she knows …

"I am not rejected. I am chosen."

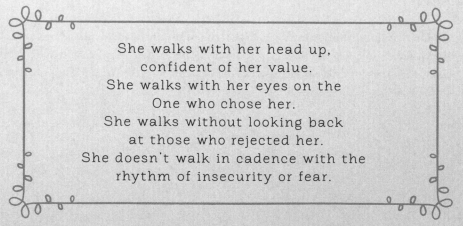

She walks with her head up,
confident of her value.
She walks with her eyes on the
One who chose her.
She walks without looking back
at those who rejected her.
She doesn't walk in cadence with the
rhythm of insecurity or fear.

She knows who she is. And it affects the kind of steps she takes and how she takes them. It affects the kinds of choices she makes and the relationships she allows. If affects the expression on her face and the words on her lips.

Do you see what I'm talking about? "I am holy" means you can walk without shame or regret over past guilt. "I have an inheritance" means you don't need to go chasing cheap substitutes in search of your worth or your future security.

You weren't made to walk in the mindless, haphazard way that many others do. You were created with a different cadence in mind by a God who has changed your identity. So even when others fall behind or even when others fall away, you can feel confident enough to walk alone, if necessary. Walk differently. Walk with purpose. Walk like you mean it. Walk without fear. Walk like you're headed to a destination worth going. Walk with resolute confidence and boldness in "who you are" and in "what you have."

You've got it!

Now go strut your stuff, girl.

INHERITING A LIFESTYLE

> You should no longer live as the Gentiles
> live, in the futility of their thoughts.
> **EPHESIANS 4:17**

THERE'S A BEAUTIFUL couple I know from our community who've been married for nearly fifty years. You'd love them. They're an uncanny mix of the traditional and the eccentric, blended together into a gorgeous relationship that's both entertaining and inspiring to watch. They're as warm and welcoming as anyone you could meet. And though they are quite modest and understated in their appearance, the truth is: they are filthy stinking rich.

Recently, they shared some upsetting news with me. They told me they've made the crushing decision–for now at least–to remove one of their children as beneficiaries to their financial legacy. They're heartbroken about it. But they have no choice, they believe. This child of theirs is living in blatant contradiction to biblical truth and is dishonoring the name of the Lord. On top of that, their child's past irresponsible business dealings lead them to believe that any inherited money would be wasted and misused. It's a matter of both faith and stewardship. They're obviously in prayer that this situation will change. It's not what they want. This is their child's inheritance. But if things remain the same, this loved one will not be able to benefit from it.

The word "Gentiles" in Scripture is often used in an ethnic sense to identify people outside the Jewish nation. It is also used (like in Ephesians 4) as a descriptive label of someone who is outside Christ and has no relationship with Him.

Turn to Ephesians 4:1-3. List some of the qualities that correspond with a Christian's identity.

Read Ephesians 4:17-19, which I've included for you. While you're reading, underline the descriptions that point to *thinking patterns*. Circle the ones that deal with *heart and emotions*. Place a box around the ones that are descriptive of *actions and behavior*.

> Live no longer as the Gentiles do, for they are hopelessly confused. Their minds are full of darkness; they wander far from the life God gives because they have closed their minds and hardened their hearts against him. They have no sense of shame. They live for lustful pleasure and eagerly practice every kind of impurity.
> **EPHESIANS 4:17-19 (NLT)**

In the second half of his letter to the Ephesians, the apostle Paul urged his readers (and now urges us) to make sure they keep themselves in position for gaining full access to their inheritance. All of these riches are available to us because of our relationship with God, but whether or not we get full use of them is determined by the lifestyle we choose. And Paul, in Ephesians 4, painted a picture of what this should look like by first painting a picture of what it shouldn't.

In the middle column of the chart below, record any way you've seen these ungodly thoughts, emotions, or behaviors play out around you recently. Leave the right-hand column blank for now. We'll come back to this later.

Unbeliever's Behavior	Example	My Behavior
Confusion		
Darkened mind		
Wandering feet		
Hardened heart		
No sense of shame		
Pleasure-seeking		
Impurity		

There was once a time when even nonbelievers in society generally respected and honored the principles of the Bible and Christianity. (The Ten Commandments, for example.) Though perhaps not professing Christ, most people's basic sense of morality still lined up with biblical teaching, loosely at least.

Not anymore.

Little sister, you are living in a *post-Christian* era. Have you ever heard that term? It's used to describe a culture in which values and worldviews are not aligned with the Christian faith. Decades ago, even people who weren't Christians recognized and respected the Bible's moral code. Today, this is no longer the case. There is a hardness toward God and His Word. People are confused and darkened in their thinking, calling spiritual ignorance a sort of enlightened freedom. There is a propensity toward wandering away from the church and the beliefs that were once the cornerstone of the community. There is a lack of shame—the loss of our gag reflex—at lifestyles and compromises that previous generations would never have tolerated. (What would my grandmother say!) There is a hunger for selfish pleasure with no real restraint pulling back against it. And there is not only a fascination with impurity, but a pressure to post and applaud and celebrate it as a part of what we consider normal social interaction.

Do you see Ephesians 4:17-19 taking place just about everywhere you look? Every day?

Such is life in a post-Christian era.

But what we need is to be shaken up by the reminder of Ephesians 4:20: "That is not how you came to know Christ."

Turn to Ephesians 4:20 and underline it in your Bible.

God is still God.

Sin is still sin.

Holiness still matters.

And Jesus is still the only way.

We serve a God who has never changed, and we live by principles that never grow post-Christian, no matter how post-Christian our society becomes. I realize you will often stand alone when you stand your ground and determine to walk differently. But a bountiful spiritual inheritance, directly tied to your identity, is what's out there for you to experience when you "walk in a manner worthy of the calling with which you have been called" (Eph. 4:1, NASB).

Go back to the chart you've been filling out today. In the right-hand column, write down some behaviors or mind-sets that contradict the ones you've already recorded there. Notice I've topped the third column with the heading "My Behavior"—because I know this is the way you're committed to walking.

Considering the chart and the point of today's study, ask God's Spirit to reveal to you any ways where you're living out of character with your identity in these areas. Write anything the Lord brings to your mind below.

Your new identity should prompt a new lifestyle. Your life should reflect your gratitude for all the Lord has done for you. You're able to live now with the mind-set, attitude, and actions He inspires you to pursue in His Word. You can dare to be markedly different from a lot of other people at your school. When you share your ideas, when you react to difficult situations, you should sound and look like someone who knows exactly who she is.

Because you're His kid. You have a calling. And when you honor Him with your lifestyle, you'll sense an abundance of His divine blessing and favor. It's your inheritance cashing out— peace that passes understanding, joy unspeakable, strength for difficult times, courage and hope, and protection against the enemy.

It's all yours. Because you are His.

And you're walking that way.

SOMETHING NEW

Put on the new self, the one created according to God's
likeness in righteousness and purity of the truth.
EPHESIANS 4:24

A FEW WEEKS AGO I shared with you about our family's trip to India. But I didn't tell you about the clothes I wore. One of the highlights of being there, really, was getting to wear traditional Indian clothing while I spoke. The women in the local church knew I'd be better received by the audience if I showed honor to their customary style of dress.

Well, in case you didn't know, in India women often wear a garment called a *sari* (pronounced like "sorry" in an American apology). They handcrafted a beautiful one for me, made of delectable fabrics in a bright green color trimmed with gold accents. But to my Dallas, Texas, style it didn't look like a dress at all when I first laid eyes on it. There weren't any holes for my head and arms, no little tidy zipper in the back. Instead it hung in loose waves of flat material. How was I supposed to put this thing on?

Turns out, I didn't *need* to know. Donning a sari requires a precise wrapping process mastered by the women of India. So while I dutifully removed my jeans and T-shirt, a lovely Indian woman wrapped the sari intricately around my body, using large pins to secure it in strategic gatherings, before finishing it all off with one last drape that cascaded elegantly over my shoulder. I felt like a queen.

I'll come back to this story tomorrow, because it gets a little funnier. But for now, I just want you to imagine with me, putting on this completely new garment that I'd never worn anything like before. Then let's dive into the Bible to see how God feels about us wearing new clothes.

Turn to Colossians 3:9-10. What phrases does Paul use that are similar to the portions of Ephesians 4:22-24 that I've included in the margin?

You were taught, with regard to your former way of life, to put off your old self, which is being corrupted by its deceitful desires; to be made new in the attitude of your minds; and to put on the new self, created to be like God in true righteousness and holiness.
EPHESIANS 4:22-24 (NIV)

How do these ideas remind you of my experience with the Indian sari?

Your new identity comes with a new outfit! Taking off the old one, while putting on the new one, is something God wants you doing every single day. Just like a police officer puts on a police uniform—just like an astronaut puts on a spacesuit—your spiritual clothing helps others see who you are. It sends a message to people around you (as well as the enemy plotting your demise in spiritual places) that you belong to God. You've been bestowed with His power and authority. And you've taken on the responsibility for that relationship.

You take *off* anything that's incompatible with it; you put *on* the new clothes that fit you.

Slowly and prayerfully comb through the Ephesians 4 and Colossians 3 passages I've printed for you here. Underline the behaviors you need to take off in order to dress in a way that fits with your new life in Christ. Circle behaviors you should put on.

Putting away lying, speak the truth, each one to his neighbor, because we are members of one another. Be angry and do not sin. Don't let the sun go down on your anger, and don't give the devil an opportunity. Let the thief no longer steal. Instead, he is to do honest work with his own hands, so that he has something to share with anyone in need. No foul language should come from your mouth, but only what is good for building up someone in need, so that it gives grace to those who hear. And don't grieve God's Holy Spirit. You were sealed by him for the day of redemption. Let all bitterness, anger and wrath, shouting and slander be removed from you, along with all malice. And be kind and compassionate to one another, forgiving one another, just as God also forgave you in Christ.
EPHESIANS 4:25-32

Put to death what belongs to your earthly nature: sexual immorality, impurity, lust, evil desire, and greed, which is idolatry. Because of these, God's wrath is coming upon the disobedient, and you once walked in these things when you were living in them. But now, put away all the following: anger, wrath, malice, slander, and filthy language from your mouth. Do not lie to one another,
COLOSSIANS 3:5-9

Looking back at the words you underlined, pick two of these old-clothes attributes you've been "wearing," and list them below.

1.

2.

Why do you find these articles of spiritual "clothing" so appealing to wear around? Are they comfortable? Do they make you look impressive to those around you? Why do you keep wearing them?

Now transfer all the discarded clothing choices from the ones you underlined into the "Take Off" portion of this chart. Then create a wardrobe list of opposite fashions in the right-hand column that you'd like to start trying on.

Take Off	Put On

Looking at a chart like the one you just completed can make you feel overwhelmed. These new clothes might be an entirely different style than you're accustomed to wearing or seeing modeled by those around you. Some of them may seem a little foreign to you—kind of like a Black American girl wrapped up in an Indian sari. Your new spiritual outfit could even make you stand out in ways you'd sort of prefer not to be recognized. I understand. Despite the popular notion that says people will celebrate you for trying to be your own unique self, you actually live in a world suffocating under a shroud of uniformity of the worst kind. But you aren't supposed to fit in. This is not your home. You're made to be different.

But you can do this, my friend. Replacing your old behaviors and thought patterns with ones that authentically look the part of your new identity is something you can accomplish through deliberate, consistent, Holy Spirit empowered effort. In fact, not only *can* you do it—let me be more clear—you *must* do it, so that you can coordinate your spiritual clothes with your new spiritual location, where you're seated in heavenly places. This holy outfit was made with you in mind. And over time, you'll find you're not only becoming more accustomed to it, but you can't imagine wearing anything else.

Your identity and your inheritance fit you perfectly.

FASHION ADVISOR

Where there is no guidance the people fall, but
in abundance of counselors there is victory.
PROVERBS 11:14 (NASB)

YESTERDAY I TOLD YOU about my experience with the gorgeous fashions of India. Gorgeous, yes. Easy to walk in? Not so much. After being fitted with my new clothes that day, I left my hotel room feeling like I'd been stuffed inside a burrito. My whole body was wrapped from head to toe in rich, velvety fabric.

The kind woman who'd gotten me meticulously wrapped insisted that she stay close beside me all evening—an idea I wasn't exactly too crazy about at first. I mean, I couldn't understand why I needed her shadowing me. I was a big girl and could take care of myself.

But as the evening unfolded, I realized I couldn't have been more wrong. Simply *walking* in the sari required lots of practice and help. I was used to the traditional Western clothing I'd grown up wearing, but this was completely different. Going up and down stairs, walking across the stage where I was presenting, even (ahem!) going to the bathroom required some wise counsel on how to navigate the flowing fabric. And, yes, she even went in *there* with me. I would have never gotten those gazillion perfectly placed pins back in position without her.

By the end of the night, I was thrilled to have had the hands-on help of my sweet Indian sister near me every step of the way. Having a coach who had experience with this attire was not just helpful, but necessary for me to be able to navigate this all-new experience.

Yesterday you wrote down two areas of behavior or attitudes that you need to "take off" in order to commit to your new identity. As you seek to "put on" a new way of life, list the names of any spiritually mature women in your life who consistently offer you encouragement and accountability. (If you don't have a name to write down, that's okay. Just leave it blank for now.)

What kinds of pitfalls might you avoid if you receive good advice from another person?

Becoming accustomed to your new life in Christ and dressing appropriately for it requires encouragement and accountability. In order for you to begin walking according to your new identity on a consistent basis, you need the reliable support of someone who knows how to wear these spiritual clothes already, who's been wearing them for a while herself, and who can show you how to walk well inside them. Just like I needed a "fashion advisor" to teach me how to wear that Indian sari, we all need someone more experienced to walk with us on our journey of faith.

The Bible is actually full of examples where one individual helped shape the life and calling of another. All throughout the Old and New Testament, we see people willing to invest their experiences and maturity in someone else.

> **Choose one or two of the following passages to study. Record your thoughts about the relationship between these two individuals. What did the older person help the younger person accomplish or understand? How did his or her influence shape the other's life?**
>
> **Exodus 18:13-26 (Jethro and Moses)**
>
> **Ruth 2:17-23 (Naomi and Ruth)**
>
> **1 Samuel 3:1-10 (Eli and Samuel)**
>
> **Luke 1:30-45 (Elizabeth and Mary)**
>
> **2 Timothy 1:1-14 (Paul and Timothy)**

Listen to me—life is hard. As a young woman in a culture that often disregards your clear stand for Christ and tries to shake your confidence in the purpose for which you were created, you need encouragement. When you're tempted and drawn into sin, someone needs permission from you to call you out and set you straight. When you're hurting and sad, when you're lonely and unsure, you need someone with whom you feel safe telling your struggles, someone whose heart is tender toward you, who will walk with you and keep you hemmed in to God's truth.

If you stop listening to correction, my son [or daughter], you will stray from the words of knowledge.
PROVERBS 19:27

But there's a key to opening up these blessings that God intends to pass from one spiritual sister to another. It is the one critical element that enables you to learn from another's wisdom, internalize the truths they share, and experience the growth their counsel is intended to produce in you.

The key is …

Read the challenge from Romans 12:16 in the margin and compare it with 1 Peter 5:5-6 in your own Bible.

Record below what you think is the key, without which you'll never be able to absorb as much as you could learn from a mentor.

Live in harmony with each other. Don't be too proud to enjoy the company of ordinary people. And don't think you know it all!
ROMANS 12:16 (NLT)

In what ways has pride made you unwilling to listen to someone else's wiser, more experienced voice in your life before?

In what areas do you tend to "think you know it all"?

I am so grateful to the Lord that He's allowed me to walk with you through almost six full weeks of Bible study so far. I feel honored to engage with you on matters as personally important to you as your identity, and that you've let me go through your closet with you, sorting out the kinds of spiritual clothes that look so good on you while getting rid of some of the stuff that, uh-uh, is just not you.

But pretty soon, you'll turn the last page and move on. That's why I want you thinking today—a couple of weeks before we're finished here—about someone you can invite to circle into your life in a personal, practical way, someone who can speak wisdom into your heart, point you in the direction of God's will, and listen to your concerns at every step.

I'll admit to you: I too often have let pride keep me from the full benefit of this experience, especially when I was your age. I've thought about what other women could do for me, like the lady in India who was so certain I needed her, and I've been sure I could take care of myself just fine without their help. But I was wrong. And if I could go back and tell my teenage self something she really needed to hear, one of the strongest words of all would be what I'd say to you, little sister: "Humble [yourself] in the sight of the Lord, and He will lift you up" (Jas. 4:10, NKJV).

Do you recall my asking you earlier to name someone you consistently seek out for encouragement and accountability? If you didn't know a name to write down, I challenge you to end your study today by doing something I finally did when I was a younger woman like you. I made it a matter of prayer. I asked the Lord to align my life with other women who could serve as mentors to me. And He answered my request in ways I could never have imagined, giving me incredible women to be my teachers. Many of them were people I'd known for years, but I'd been too full of myself to notice them until God opened my spiritual eyes to see them.

I suspect if you'll ask Him, He'll do the same thing for you.

SHARP DRESSERS

The one who walks with the wise will become wise,
but a companion of fools will suffer harm.
PROVERBS 13:20

NEAR THE END of my first semester at college, one of my dearest, lifelong friends came to visit. Jada and I hadn't seen each other in months, and we started our weekend of fun by—what else?—shopping! We went from one store to another in quick succession, just grabbing clothes off the rack, darting in and out of dressing rooms, and then laughing or commenting on each other's choices.

At one point, I came out wearing a mid-thigh skirt and pranced over to the mirror while Jada stood behind me, noticeably silent. "What? You don't like it?" I asked—checking myself out, glancing back at her, trying to interpret this mysterious look she was giving me.

"Pri-SCILL-a!" she finally blurted out, as if seeing me poured into this tiny mini skirt had made it too difficult for her to contain herself any longer. "Girl, that skirt is way too short! Your mom would never let you wear that! And you probably shouldn't let you wear it either."

She was right. There in that mirror, I saw the skirt. I'd looked at it in the dressing room before coming out to show her, but I didn't see it clearly until her honesty opened up my eyes.

We all need honest, loving friends like that—the kind who will reach around and fix your collar if it's standing up weird in the back—the kind who will tell you when you've got a little sprig of lunch stuck between your teeth—the kind who care more about you than about how you feel about them. They tell you the truth. They shoot you straight. Because they love you. For real.

Yesterday we talked about the importance of having mentors in your life to help keep you encouraged in walking out your identity. But equally important are the people who surround you. You need peers who will speak truth to you in love—sisters who are brave enough to open your eyes to self-realities you haven't been willing to face. These kinds of relationships contribute heavily to the mindsets that govern you, the behaviors that shape you, and the habits that become part of your daily life.

While we tend not to proactively seek mentoring relationships at all, the more common problem with same-age friends and acquaintances is that we're not as careful and discerning as we should be with who we allow to become our most intimate influencers. We need to get better at this and choose our friends wisely.

What's the word picture painted by the writer of Proverbs 27:17 in the margin?

Iron sharpens iron, and one person sharpens another.
PROVERBS 27:17

List some practical ways this dynamic appears between you and your closest friends.

Write your name in the center circle of the chart below. In the blank circles around it, list the names of close friends who influence you in a *good* way.

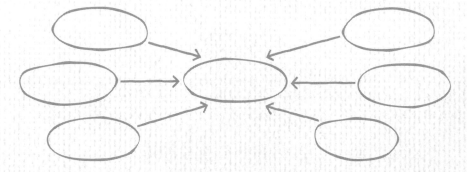

Near each name, write an example of how that particular friend "sharpens" you.

Relationships worth having are the kind that keep you sharp in the Spirit. These God-friends may be few and far between, but they're the ones who help you prioritize your new fashion sense. They'll help you clearly see any areas where you need to modify your attitudes or behaviors, so the clothing of holiness fits well. They will gently make you aware of the misshapen parts of your life, brought on by the overconsumption of unhealthy choices that you may not be aware of (or might be ignoring). And they'll give you pep talks that keep you confident and encouraged as you seek to honor God. They also won't *dis*courage you or make you feel strange because of your countercultural choices regarding the entertainment you indulge, the media you consume, and the type of relationships you allow in your life.

Consider 1 Corinthians 15:33 in the margin. How have you witnessed "bad company" corrupting "good morals" in your life?

Do not be deceived: "Bad company corrupts good morals."
1 CORINTHIANS 15:33

From the following partial list of lifestyle decisions warned against in Scripture, record how you and your friends may actually make them easier on each other to avoid.

Stealing:

Anger:

Promiscuity:

Bad language:

Gossip:

Lying:

Greed:

You may not feel like doing this, but I think it's important for you to consider it. In the space below, write the names of anyone you spend time with, whose influence steers you toward these types of behaviors and attitudes and *away* from a life that honors God.

How does your relationship with this person need to change?

How do you expect her to respond if you put certain restrictions in place?

Why does your love for her, your kindness toward her, and your desire for her greatest welfare demand that you do this?

To be clear, none of us are perfect or superior to others in our value to the Lord. Like my 17-year-old friend Ellie says, "I'm not better; I've just decided to make better choices." But we need help, not hindrances. We are too blind and weak on our own unless others are helping us see and helping us walk. Not even the church is a perfect place. It's not filled with perfect people. But it's vital that you stay connected there. The church is the community your heavenly Father has created for His children to gather for the purpose of (at least in part) encouraging one another.

Read Hebrews 10:24-25. What do these verses tell us to be concerned with?

What should be the tone of our relationships with brothers and sisters in Christ?

According to a recent study, *two-thirds* of American young adults who attended church regularly for at least a year as teenagers say they dropped out of church for at least a year between the ages of 18 and 22.[2] This tells me many young adults no longer view church as a viable and necessary place to build a community of like-minded Christian friends.

But it should be. It *must* be, if you truly expect to walk out your identity. I'm not just talking about attending the weekly service when your church meets for worship. I'm talking about living life with God-friends who are plugged into the larger body of Christ, whether they go to the church you're a part of, or whether they are planted in an entirely different location and denomination. They serve, learn, and value God's people and God's house. We are part of a Christian community scattered across the entire world. And we *need* each other. They *need* you, and you need them.

> **In your peer group, what are the overarching feelings you hear expressed about church and its relevance? If needed, how can you use what you've learned today to help change the conversation?**

Some of my most special, same-age friends today are women I met when I was a teen. Not all of us live in the same state anymore. Not all of us come from the same church background or share the same racial ethnicity. Still, we've kept each other accountable through the years, and we're still actively doing it. We encourage one another, we challenge one another, and we help one another keep our moral compasses pointed true north. This kind of a sisterhood can impact your life in ways you'd never imagine for many years to come.

> **Ask the Lord to open your eyes to any sister, from anywhere, that He might entrust you to befriend, so you can encourage each other to put on your new spiritual clothes and walk like young women who know how to wear them.**

WE'VE WORKED through some pretty big pieces of biblical and practical truth this week, and I hope you've been able to make some new commitments that'll create significant changes in your life, in regard to:

- Learning how to walk.
- Taking off the old and putting on the new.
- Seeking older, wiser women to help you learn how to live.
- Being intentional and careful about your circle of friends.
- Remaining a committed part of the body of Christ, no matter how unimportant others may think the church is or is becoming.

Don't be discouraged if these realities develop slowly, over time. Just continue to make intentional progress. Obey and honor God even when you stumble and struggle through some of these lifestyle and thinking adjustments. God's Spirit is committed to making you sharper and more effective and to giving you the victory that is rightfully yours. As you remain faithful to Him through each season of your life, He'll even use the difficult and boring parts of your journey as ways of continuing to mold and fashion you into the image of your Father.

And if I didn't say it clearly enough before, I want to take this shortened "half day" to reiterate to you that I understand how difficult it can be to live a life that goes against culture. It's always been difficult, but perhaps never more of a challenge than it is today.

Read Ephesians 5:1-4. What does God's Word call His people to do?

What are some things, according to this passage, that "should not even be heard of among you"?

How would these challenges from Scripture, if you really took them to heart, lead to making some tough choices concerning:

- **your use of social media?**

- the words you say to others or about others?

- your decisions about what to laugh at and condone?

Those are not easy choices to make. But they are the *right* choices to make. And the reason you know they're right is because they square up with "who you are." They're reflective of "what you have."

They correspond to your identity and your inheritance.

As you begin to proactively do the things we've studied this week–walk differently, "dress" differently, listen to different people, and interact with others differently–you will become more prepared for the journey ahead. Even if you're standing alone, you'll be standing firm–full of faith and assurance and on the side of freedom.

This week, I am praying for you. Praying that God would open your eyes, more each day, to see who you are. Praying that He would communicate to you through His Word and His Spirit how you can apply your identity to your everyday life. Praying that He'd peel away any people or influences from your life who are not helping you grow and mature spiritually (and that you'd be brave enough to let them go). And praying that you'll stay encouraged, especially when it's difficult and unpopular, to stay true to what you believe.

I am so proud of you. You're a courageous young lady. And there's a whole lot of us standing behind you and cheering you on.

IN CHRIST, ON PURPOSE

The Holy Spirit of God lives in you to _____ you to _____ who God has called you to be and _____ what God has called you to do.

List a few accomplishments of David:

Does God's will seem to be an idea that is on hold for the future?

Being in God's _____ looks like engaging fully in the _____ that He has set before you to do today.

How does it change the way you react and respond to real life when you realize you are serving the purposes of God in your everyday life?

Having purpose changes _____ .

You are on mission _____ _____ .

This generation has been _____ to you.

DARLENE HAD a difficult childhood. She had placed faith in Jesus and was raised in church, but it wasn't a healthy, thriving environment. Instead, she often felt held to a legalistic standard of religion that made her feel shame and fear more than freedom and joy. To her, being a Christ follower felt gloomy and glowering, heavy and hovering and, honestly, pretty hypocritical.

To top it off, when she was a teenager someone she trusted from church took advantage of her sexually. The emotional and physical devastation was overwhelming. She felt hurt. She felt confused. She felt even more hardened toward the church and toward the possibility of Jesus being her friend and redeemer. As a result, weighed down by this underlying, ever-present sense of inferiority and failure, she latched onto anything and anyone that made her feel worthy. It led to a slew of admittedly poor choices. At some point, I guess, she simply quit caring.

But then something changed. A shift began to take place. And today, as we move into our last full week of study, I want us to paint this change that Darlene experienced–the change that you and I can experience–in its true colors, helping you see more clearly how your new identity becomes your walk, your lifestyle, and then your whole mission in life.

Every human being is made up of three elements: spirit, soul, and body.[1]
- Your *spirit* is the core and inmost essence of who you are, made for relationship with God.
- Your *soul* is home to your unique nature–your thoughts, ambitions, feelings, conscience. It's your personality.
- Your *body* is the physical, temporary container for all of these immaterial elements.

> **In the center circle of the diagram on page 157, write the words "HOLY SPIRIT" in all caps above the words "human spirit."**

> **Take a brightly colored pencil and shade in the center circle.**

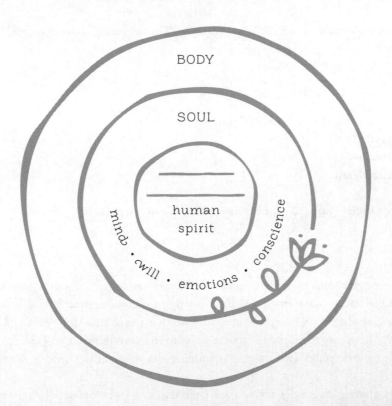

BODY

SOUL

human spirit

mind · will · emotions · conscience

The reason I asked you to add "Holy Spirit" to the circle containing "human spirit" is to indicate they're not the same thing. You and I were born with a human spirit that, although designed for connection with God, was deadened by sin. Not until you became a believer in Jesus Christ did the Holy Spirit take up residence in you, sparking your dead "human spirit" to life. The old has gone and the new has come.

Now if you truly expect your *mind* (your thoughts and attitudes), your *will* (your desires and decisions), your *emotions* (your feelings and reactions), your *conscience* (your awareness of right and wrong), and even the actions of your physical *body* to reflect the change that's happened at the center of you, the Holy Spirit's influence needs to ooze into all these areas of your life.

Use the same colored pencil and let it bleed now outside of that center circle, "oozing" over into those outer rings that represent the other elements of your human makeup.

If you were to choose one aspect of your thought life, your hopes, your emotions, your conscience, or your physical health that most needs to be touched by the Holy Spirit's influence right now, what would it be?

Turn to 1 Thessalonians 5:23. What does this "God of peace" want to accomplish in you?

How fully is He able to "sanctify" you?
    A. partially
    B. nearly
    C. completely

In what specific areas of your life does He desire to complete it?

Darlene, through a ministry on her college campus, began to learn about the truths you've studied today. She learned that the Holy Spirit was willing and able to sanctify her whole being, transforming every aspect of her and that she should stop resisting Him and cooperate in the process. She began to surrender to the sanctification process and slowly and steadily, she began to detect a reprogramming and reformatting process taking place.

She started *thinking* differently, aware she'd been wrong about what she thought would make her happy. She started *desiring* differently, not wanting to be promiscuous and dishonoring to her body anymore. She started *feeling* differently, developing a tenderness in her heart toward the church and other Christians. She could tell she was becoming more at peace with herself and her circumstances. She was even able to offer forgiveness to the one who'd taken advantage of her, which in turn ushered her into a newfound freedom. She was becoming …

Well, different.

And that's what will happen in your life, as you keep allowing the truth of God's Word, working through the power of God's Spirit, to repaint your whole life in the colors of your new identity.

But not only does the Holy Spirit change how you live each day by influencing your individual choices and behaviors and transforming your patterns of thinking, He also sets you on a course of life that can only be described as your mission. More than merely watching old sinful habits become steady patterns of obedience–switching negatives to positives–you can start seeing your love for God multiply into an active, hungry passion for serving Him.

Turn quickly to Romans 5 in your Bible. Verses 1-2 reiterate some of the blessings that come to you through salvation. Do you spot any words that match up with some of the "who you are" and "what you have" descriptors of your identity? List a few.

Now move down to verses 3-5. What else does God begin producing in your heart as He keeps working through your life circumstances? Unscramble the following answers:

D U R E A N E C N : _____

C R T E C R A H A : _____

P O H E : _____

Who does verse 5 say is responsible for producing and escalating these virtues in your life?

" … the H_____ S_____ who was _____ to us."

Living your identity is so much more than just becoming a better person or fitting into a mold that all good Christians are supposed to look like. It is letting the love of God, poured into your heart through the Holy Spirit, pour out into your soul and body—and pour out so completely that everything you do, for the rest of your life, becomes drenched in it, brimming over with it.

Let's close with how one of the psalm writers described it.

> Happy are the people whose strength is in you.…
> They go from strength to strength…
> PSALM 84:5-7

And this is where you're going. "From strength to strength." Living on mission with the Holy Spirit, your lifelong source and supply.

EXTRA SERVING

"Whoever wants to become great among
you will be your servant,"
MARK 10:43

I'M ALWAYS DAZZLED by women who live purposefully and intentionally. I'm inspired by sisters who make ongoing daily choices—sometimes difficult ones—to carry out the responsibilities pressed upon them during each season of their lives. They're not perfect, but they are intentional, because they realize their choices have eternal consequences. Instead of living carelessly, instead of living selfishly, they make choices that constantly bear in mind their divine mission.

But even more beautiful, to me, is when women live out these types of commitments despite having a history of past mistakes and missteps. They're still dealing with painful memories, sure. They're still bearing the scars of some tough consequences. And yet they believe to their core the loving, redemptive words that God spoke over His people in ancient times: "Do not be afraid, for you will not be put to shame; don't be humiliated, for you will not be disgraced" (Isa. 54:4).

So they walk into God's grace and peace. They bravely receive by faith the new identity He has given them. Not only do they refuse to live as they once did; they begin to seek out new opportunities to stretch and expand their spiritual muscles. They look to God, not to themselves, for direction and clarity. They look to His Word, not their own desires, to lead the way each day. They still have fun, but not by sacrificing their God-given priorities.

And I've just got to say—these women inspire me. Mission-minded women. I've always wanted to be a woman like that.

I want you to be a woman like that, too.

> **Complete the following sentence in your own words: "A young woman living a purposeful, mission-minded life is someone who ... "**

> **List the names of any peers or older women who inspire you with their mission-mindedness.**

Write a short description or example spotlighting the main aspects of their lives that impress you the most.

We've spent the last few weeks looking at the kinds of changes God can empower you to make based on the realities of your identity in Christ. New clothes. A new walk. Out with the old, and in with the new creation. All of that is amazing, and I hope you're experiencing the fresh air of your Spirit-inspired obedience.

It feels really good, doesn't it?

But what if I told you it gets even better? This new walk of yours is about to become a journey, an adventure, an everyday wonder at what God is going to do next, taking your life in the direction of His pre-planned purposes, which are beyond your wildest imaginations.

Let's take your identity to the next level.

Let's go out on mission.

Underline the most inspiring components of the verses in the margin.

Write down any observations or desires that come to mind when seeing how the Bible summarizes David's life.

"I have found David the son of Jesse to be a man after my own heart, who will carry out all my will."
ACTS 13:22

"David, after serving God's purpose in his own generation..."
ACTS 13:36

King David, you might already know, was not a perfect man, but he was an intentional man. He had his highs and lows—sometimes selfish and sinful, but often humble and honoring of Yahweh. Still, he appears not once, but twice in Paul's concise history of God's people in Acts 13, and he's remembered for what made him special. He's remembered for what you, too—despite the highs and lows—can embody as you live out God's mission for your life.

Today, I want to focus on only one aspect: David's *service*.

He served. He was servant-hearted. He served the purposes of God.

Your mission, no matter its personal details, must be marked by a heart that is focused on being a servant of God.

What adjectives would you use to describe someone who serves?

What would you say is the main focus or goal of someone who is a servant?

Turn to Mark 10. From verses 35-37, what did two of Jesus' followers ask Him to do for them?

What would compel them to ask such a thing?

From verse 41, how do we feel when we see self-serving attitudes in others?

From verses 42-45, what does Jesus include as our calling, our mission?

"For even the Son of Man did not come to be served, but to serve, and to give his life as a ransom for many."
MARK 10:45

How many ways did He model a servant's heart Himself?

Every season of David's life required different responsibilities, necessitating the use of different skills and talents. And yet no matter what specific role he was filling–from young age to old age and every age in between–"serving God's purpose" was his overarching mission. Whether he was tending sheep, playing music, writing poetry, or ruling a kingdom, his main goal was serving the Lord.

This is what servants do. They are not self-serving. Instead, in every task and season of life they are looking for opportunities to accomplish God's purposes and bring glory to His name.

If anyone serves, let it be from the strength God provides, so that God may be glorified through Jesus Christ in everything.
1 PETER 4:11

In your own season of life today, you're a student, a daughter, a single woman, a friend. Perhaps you're a sister, a techie, a blogger, a musician, an athlete, an artist, a leader. Soon enough the seasons of your life will change, and you'll become your own unique combination of possibilities: maybe a business owner, wife, mother, ministry leader, among various other roles and responsibilities. But during each time frame, within each ingredient, your commitment to the mission can be the same as David's.

Fill in the blank: My name is _____, and in every season of my life, my goal is to _____ the purposes of God in my generation.

Ask the Lord to give you His perspective for how you can use the different aspects of your life to serve His goals and accomplish His mission. Choose any three of your personal roles that describe yourself at the current time. Underneath each one, list three ways you could be "on mission"—serving as you do that task.

As a _____, I can be a true servant by:

1,

2.

3.

As a _____, I can be a true servant by:

1.

2.

3.

As a _____, I can be a true servant by:

1.

2.

3.

Now go into the day that's stretched out before you and live this way. It's what servant-hearted, mission-minded young women, like you, do.

WEEK 7 · DAY 2
THE RIGHT CONSISTENCY

"I have set my face like flint, and I know
I will not be put to shame."
ISAIAH 50:7

ANYBODY WHO becomes a king–a royal–obviously ends up living a pretty exciting life, different from the rest of us. But thanks to David's large storyline in the Bible, we get to see a lot more of his life than just the king part. Let's go inside that timeline a little deeper.

No one is completely positive of the exact date when David was born. It was likely in the neighborhood of 1040 BC. There's general agreement that he was roughly around sixteen years old when Samuel anointed him king of Israel (approx. 1024 BC), but his actual reign didn't begin for another thirteen years or so. The accepted dates of his rule began in 1011 BC and ran through 971 BC, a period of forty years.

This timeline represents the years between David's birth and his official reign as king. Notice the other blank spaces above and below the line. We'll come back to them in a few minutes.

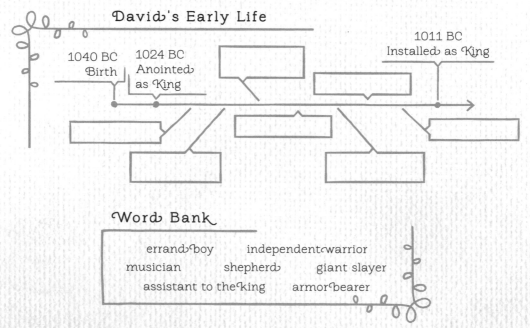

Before we complete the timeline, look at the chart on the following page. Using the Scripture references, as well as the accompanying word bank, match David's job descriptions with the verses where they appear. Also write them into the blanks around the timeline.

1 Samuel 16:11	
1 Samuel 16:16-18	
1 Samuel 16:21	
1 Samuel 17:17-20	
1 Samuel 17:45-48	
1 Samuel 18:5	
1 Samuel 22:1-2	

Notice that all these job descriptions were true of David *before* 1011 BC, before he became king and before he even reached about thirty years of age. Look at the wide variety of jobs–some mundane and underwhelming (errand boy); others a bit more prestigious, notable, and challenging (giant slayer). He was willing to take on all kinds of tasks *before* he was recognized by others as a noteworthy person. He didn't consider himself too good for the boring ones, nor did he consider himself too young or immature for the more challenging ones. He certainly didn't sit around doing nothing until "something better" came along. He remained a consistent servant of God while tending sheep for his dad, while strumming a musical instrument for King Saul, and while being a gofer for his older brothers. It was all significant to him. Why? Because he had a higher mission in mind–serving the purposes of God in his generation.

Consider this important fact: he already knew (along with only a handful of others) that he was destined by God to be king to the whole nation, many years before it happened. In that light, his patience and contentment in these interim roles appears even more remarkable. He knew–he *knew*–a throne was waiting for him, and yet no job was too small that he didn't remain steadily committed to his main mission of serving God in the meantime, whether it meant being a disrespected kid or even an underling to the man who sat on David's rightful throne.

He waited.

He did whatever task was in front of him.

And he did it consistently, with patience, not getting ahead of himself, but trusting that the Lord would honor David's heart and effort.

He stayed *consistently* on mission. Consistency matters.

What are the parts of your life—your jobs, roles, and assignments—that perhaps you're not overly happy about at present?

Why do you feel this way? Are they boring? Do they feel beneath you? Are they embarrassing in comparison to what others are doing or what you wish you were doing?

If you're not happy right now with the way your mission in life is looking, how do you think David would tell you to respond to it?

Let's go up in rank far above David now. Let's go all the way to Jesus' example when He came here to carry out His own mission on earth. Jesus, you know, was a member of the Trinity–God Himself. Talk about a step-down from His rightful position. When He looked into the eyes of people who didn't agree with Him or didn't appreciate Him–even those who outright despised Him and everything He stood for–they were looking into the eyes of the One who created them. How about that? *They* didn't know it (or wouldn't believe it), but *He* knew it.

And yet despite living so far beneath His deserving dignity, He stayed humble enough to be consistent with His overarching mission.

Jesus explained, "I tell you the truth, the Son can do nothing by himself. He does only what he sees the Father doing. Whatever the Father does, the Son also does."
JOHN 5:19 (NLT)

Read John 5:19 in the margin. Underline the portions that stand out most to you.

Use this space to explain why these statements Jesus made are so meaningful to you.

Jesus called Himself the Son, meaning He willingly submitted Himself to a higher authority, looking to the Father alone for cues about what He should do and when He should do it. He also determined that no matter what kinds of twists and turns His life presented to Him along the way to

His mission's fulfillment, He would do anything–anything at all–if that's where He saw evidence of His Father's hand at work.

If you're interested in reading these Servant Songs (as they're commonly called), see Isaiah 42:1-9; 49:1-13; 50:4-11; 52:13–53:12.

Turn to Isaiah 50:7. This is part of a passage that, like several others in Isaiah, is considered prophetic of Jesus. What did He know the Lord would do for Him?

What did He know the Lord would *never* do to Him?

What did He determine to do, based on these truths?

Jesus' mission was to honor the Father, so He "set [His] face like flint"–like a rock–to do it.

In order for us to be women who honor God and live well, we must be patient enough, humble enough, prayerful enough, and determined enough to do whatever God is leading us to do today. The hope of what we think is coming tomorrow may contribute to making today's task seem undesirable, unappealing, or unnecessary. But you're on mission. Today's work matters. And your consistency will be important in ways you cannot yet see. Like David, it will prepare you for the next things God has planned for you.

> "Well done, good and faithful servant! You were faithful over a few things; I will put you in charge of many things."
> MATTHEW 25:21

End your time of study today by converting this closing verse into a prayer of commitment. Ask the Lord to empower you, so you can remain faithful in even the smallest thing for His glory and to accomplish His mission.

YOUR BEST YOU

> He shepherded them with a pure heart and
> guided them with his skillful hands.
> *PSALM 78:72*

I'LL BE HONEST with you, I think I've had nearly as many role changes throughout my life as David did.

- In college, I was a single woman who interned as a part-time radio disc jockey.
- In my early twenties, I became a graduate student, switching fields to work in television, while leading a Bible study for ten female students at a local university.
- At twenty-four, I became a wife and switched career tracks again, speaking as a corporate trainer and developer.
- In my late twenties and early thirties, I began to sense God leading me into full-time ministry, just as my family was starting to grow. I was soon a mom and seeking to minister to other women… officially unemployed.
- A publisher invited me to put a message of mine into book format. To my great surprise, I became an author.
- Throughout my thirties, that piece of writing dovetailed into the opportunity to record Bible studies on video, even as I settled into being the Chief Operating Officer of the Shirer household—cooking, cleaning, and changing more dirty diapers than you can imagine.
- In my forties—surprise of *all* surprises—I was asked by Stephen and Alex Kendrick to consider performing in one of their upcoming films. Bam! Just like that, I became an actor.

I admit, I was caught off guard by a lot of these changes. They were often unexpected—sometimes in a difficult way, sometimes in an exciting way.

But here's what I wish I had known earlier, when I was your age. Every distinct piece of my life's puzzle was connected to another. I wish I'd realized that my faithfulness (or lack thereof) in one area would create a sturdy foundation (or not) for the next one. I wish I'd understood a holy connection existed between each season's task. My job on any given day was not simply about the *details* of what I was tasked with doing. The much greater reality was that it was all connected inside God's plans and purposes for my life's mission, the things He'd created me to accomplish. Each layer was building to the next.

And your life is the same way. Doesn't matter what today's leg of the journey involves—might be dull, might be dreary—it still has a beautiful, holy connection to where He's taking you and what He made you for, even the parts that seem the least beautiful or eternally significant. Take a look at how David's experience displays this:

Read Psalm 78:70-71 in the margin. Notice the similar language and imagery the writer uses to describe two very different jobs that David worked during his life. What's the connection he makes?

He chose David his servant and took him from the sheep pens; he brought him from tending ewes to be shepherd over his people Jacob— over Israel, his inheritance.
PSALM 78:70-71

As a young man, David was put in charge of his family's flocks. He helped them find food and good grazing land. He often needed to fend off intruders and attackers, protecting the animals entrusted to his care. I doubt, though, when David was out there in those grassy fields on long, boring days, that he ever realized these very tasks were actually preparing him to become a great king.

But weren't they? Didn't many of the skills he learned in his shepherding duties connect closely to kingship? Israel would need to be guided, guarded, and secured by an able leader. The selfless, servant heart that David developed within the sheepfold was exactly what God knew he'd need when those sheep became a nation full of people.

How else might shepherding have been a training course in governing?

Look up Psalm 78 and read verse 72. How does it describe the manner in which David "shepherded" the people?

Why would this statement probably not have been true if, during those days when he'd been a young shepherd, he hadn't done his work "with a pure heart" and "skillful hands"?

Remember yesterday, when we marked out David's varying jobs on a timeline of his life? Today, let's do the same for yours.

On the first timeline on the next page, add your birthday and today's date in the spaces provided. Then in the blanks above and below, list a few of the jobs, roles, or tasks you've done in the past or are currently doing in life.

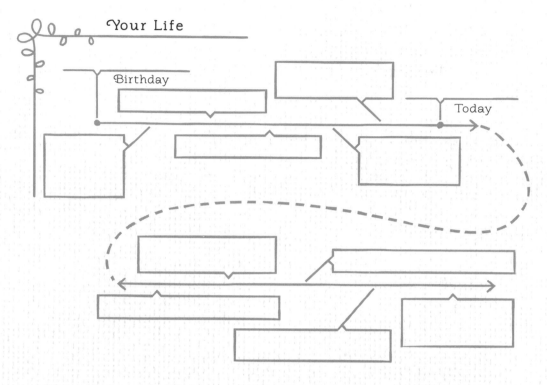

Place a checkmark beside the ones that you honestly feel like you're doing (or have done) with a "pure heart" and with "skillful hands."

For the ones you honestly couldn't check, list any reasons for why you didn't or haven't been doing those things to the best of your abilities.

On the second timeline (which represents your life from today forward), fill in what you anticipate some of your jobs or responsibilities will be in the future.

How could you foresee any of your past or current tasks as being preparation for these possible future roles?

When I look back today on the changing roles God has given me in my own life, I can't help noticing that just about everything I'm doing now is directly connected to what I was doing early on. Television, for example. I told you I did some work in TV as a journalist. What I didn't tell you was how frustrating it became to me, because the tasks I was given were, by and large, unrecognized, unappreciated, requiring little creativity on my part. I felt a bit stifled by them. I did many of them halfheartedly. I also experienced a gripping sense of insecurity and disappointment at times when my opportunities in broadcasting proved short-lived, when the news shows I reported on were canceled, and when they didn't seem to be leading toward anything significant in terms of a career direction.

But what if I'd known my success at television—whatever "success" I thought should look like—was not why God sent me down that path? What if I'd been able to see that the practice of simply becoming comfortable in front of the camera was going to be vital preparation for, let's say, taping video-driven Bible study sessions that would become such a huge part of the divine calling for which I was created? I had no idea then, but in hindsight I can see the connection clearly.

Listen, many strands of connective tissue exist between your *now* and the overall mission that God has planned for your life. Today may seem like a big waste of time. You may be dealing with an upset or disappointment, and you're thinking about just quitting. But I'm here to tell you, it's all preparation. Do it all with a pure heart and skillful hands. You'll look back and either be glad you did or you will wish you had.

Quickly turn to 1 Timothy 1:5. What did Paul identify to young Timothy as the three things he hoped to see growing in people? (Hint: one of them is what was said of David.)

What if, at the end of each day, you evaluated your performance by whether or not you moved toward these three goals?

Do everything for the glory of God, dear sister. You are on divine assignment, no matter how small its current appearance. In later years, you'll look back and see that what you're doing right now is intricately intertwined with where God has been taking you all along.

How does your identity—"who you are" and "what you have"—impact the way you approach today's opportunities for service?

Spend time talking with God about the things you're not doing with an attitude of excellence. Ask Him to shift your perspective toward anticipating the holy connections He is making in your life.

WHO, WHAT, NOW

He shepherded them with a pure heart and
guided them with his skillful hands.
PSALM 78:72

ONE OF MY FAVORITE parts of our sons' early education was teaching them how to sound out letters, then string letters together to form words, then string words together to make complete sentences.

I often reminded them that for a thought or sentence to be complete, it needed to contain both a *who* and a *what*. This was my elementary explanation for a noun and verb—a subject and a predicate. I told them no matter how many words they assembled into an impressively long line, it didn't create a sentence unless one of those words was a *who* and one of those words was a *what*.

Your identity is your *who*. I hope we've established this reality in a clear, exciting, unforgettable fashion. Getting the *who* part of yourself permanently printed on your mind and heart is critically important. In fact, you are way ahead of the game, sister, because of the time you've invested in learning who you are. Most people don't. But you aren't most people.

But a *who* needs a *what*. Your identity inhabits a mission. Just as a sentence is incomplete without both of these necessary pieces, your life will always be missing something if not for your willingness to recognize and submit to *what* God has called you to do.

The generic Christian term for this concept is *God's will*. I cannot tell you how many times I am asked a version of the following question by young women just like you:

How can I know God's will for my life?

It's a good, important question. It stems from an honorable desire to please Him. I'd much rather hear someone ask this question than not care enough to think about it at all. And, understandably, when they ask it, they're hoping for a finite, concrete answer that's as specific to their own life and circumstances as possible.

However …

I wish I could tell my younger self exactly what I want to seal into your heart right now, so you can rest easy, simply enjoying your life with the Lord.

My answer to the question, "How can I know God's will for my life?" is that God's will for your life is found in hourly increments of obedience. In other words …

Stop looking for God's will and just start living it.

Rewrite this principle below word for word as I have written it above.

Now stop for a moment and ask God to personalize it for you. (Deep breath. Let the message settle.) When you're ready, rewrite this phrase in your own words. Think of it this way: How would you explain this message to friends if you were sitting across from them over lattes and fraps at a local coffee shop?

Instead of fretting about knowing God's will, I'd rather you consider these related questions:

- **What tasks and responsibilities are in front of me today?**

- **Am I doing them or am I avoiding them?**

- **Am I honoring them in my attitudes and in my actions as I do them?**

- **Or am I doing them begrudgingly?**

Honoring God with today—by engaging in what He has set before you and walking in obedience—*is God's will for your life*! Devote your whole self to the task in front of you, and as a result you will continue to run smack dab into the purposes and plans of God. This is how mission-minded legacies are made—one day at a time, tending one sheep at a time, writing one song at a time, crafting one poem at a time, running one errand at a time. God's will is less of a big, enormous, theoretical something out there, and more of a simple, available opportunity disguised as an average day.

What has God asked you to do today? This *is* your mission. This *is* your mandate. This *is* God's will for your life. So do it to the glory of God.

Let's do one more piece of serious Bible study together. I'd like you to choose one of the following people from Scripture, then follow me on a case study through an important event from his or her life. Whichever person you pick, answer the following five questions:

1. Who is this? (What descriptions and identifying factors do you see?)

2. What are his or her circumstances? (How difficult or surprising do they look?)

3. Why might this person question whether or not he or she is in God's will?

4. What happens that indicates he or she is right in the middle of His will?

5. How is God's presence affirmed in this situation?

The information you need for uncovering each answer is contained in the Scripture passage that corresponds with the number of each question. (Each passage for each character comes from the same Bible book.)

	1	2	3	4	5
Ruth	Ruth 1:1-5.	1:11-12	1:19-22	3:1-9	4:13-17
Naaman's Servant	2 Kings 5:1-2.	5:3-6	5:10-12	5:10-12	5:16-17
Nehemiah	Nehemiah 1:1-4.	2:1-6	4:1-3	4:7-15	6:15-16
Esther	Esther 2:1-10.	3:7-10	4:8-12	4:13-14	5:1-8
Daniel	Daniel 6:1-3.	6:4-9	6:10-18	6:19-24	6:25-28

My Bible Character _____

1.

2.

3.

4.

5.

> Whatever you do, in word or in deed, do everything in the name of the Lord Jesus, giving thanks to God the Father through him.
> *COLOSSIANS 3:17*

These mostly young men and women were not superheroes. Just because their stories appear in the Bible doesn't make them any more special than you. They faced challenges that most of us know from our Bible story books—Esther and the king, Daniel and the lion's den, and so on. But in their life, in their world, these now-famous moments were simply the circumstances and decisions facing them *today*. God's will wasn't a mysterious riddle waiting to be answered somewhere in their future. God's will was in their face. God's will was in their *now*.

The legacy you're leaving for the generations that come after you is being built right now, in the hours that are spread out before you. The choices, attitudes, and endeavors you embrace for the glory of God today are preparing you for the adventure God is taking you on tomorrow.

> Stop looking for God's will and just start living it.

Here's your mission: Perform each task before you as an offering to the Lord, and watch Him fortify your character, sharpen your focus, tenderize your heart, and prune your life to yield maximum harvest for His glory. Relax. Don't worry. Don't rush. Just live. For Him.

You know *who* you are.

And now you know *what* to do.

THE MOMENT you were born was a divinely ordained point in history. From that point forward, you have been allotted a period of time by God, not just to exist, but to serve His purposes. In your generation.

This means amid the current political climate in your country, the moral lapses of your culture, the gaps of peace on this planet, the influences of art, music, and ideas that affect people's thinking and worldview–this is the generation, your generation, to influence with "who you are" and "what you have." If you commit to being a mission-minded woman, God will use your simple, daily obedience to mark this earth with His presence and purposes.

Never forget David's legacy of "serving God's purpose in his own generation" (Acts 13:36). Each generation comes with its unique set of obstacles and triumphs. From the Great Depression of the 1930s, to the Civil Rights Movement of the 1960s, to the technological explosion of the twenty-first century, mission-minded people have always intersected their lives intentionally with the cultural moments in which they lived. And the Lord has now chosen you–with all the uniqueness of your physicality and personality–to live out your mission at this particular leg of the race.

It's your turn. It's your time. Determine not to be merely a statistic in this generation, a burden to this generation, a liability of this generation. Serve it and bless it and make God great in it. You're not responsible for past generations, nor are you directly responsible for the next generation. Your divine mission is significantly and intricately tied to your generation. It's by God's design that you are here–it's by God's design that you are you–at this precise downbeat of time.

So let's do it. If you fall, get back up and start moving again. If others fall, step behind them to pick them up and cheer them on. If you start to feel your role is less important than others, remember that your purpose is God's purpose in your own generation, and stay committed to doing it in service to Him and by serving the needs of others.

As we close this week, read the following three verses:

Matthew 5:16

Romans 12:1

1 Timothy 1:12

Which verse jumped out as being the one you think God most wanted you to hear today? Go back and read that one again. Ask the Holy Spirit to open it wider to you. How does His power need to ooze through that verse's truth into your soul today—into your mind, your will, your emotions, your conscience, all the way out into your body? Write down what you hear.

Why are these insights so important for you in particular to hear, on this day, as someone living in your generation?

You do not exist within this generation by chance. You exist here in your own specific identity, bearing a new identity in Christ, to serve God's purposes in your generation. Your talents, passions, perspectives, and creativity are assigned to this hour in history.

This is your mission and mandate, little sister—not fame, not being discovered. Honoring God and living out your identity in Him is the only thing worth wanting. You are a walking, breathing advertisement for your Savior today.

Get out there. In your generation. And live it.

Week Eight

GUARDING YOUR IDENTITY

PRESS PLAY

Use the space below to follow along and take any notes as you watch the video for Week 8.

What do you find happening around you that makes it the most difficult for you to maintain your own identity in Christ?

Righteousness is a _____ .

Your heart is the hub of your _____ .

How are you going to be proactive in guarding your heart against the schemes of the enemy, and instead live to honor God?

The challenge is now to _____ to guard your _____ through every season of your life.

How will you be intentional to continually surround yourself with other women who will help you on your mission of living out your true identity?

THE OLDER I GET, the more I realize the critical importance of being an active participant with the Holy Spirit's work inside me. Salvation is free. It's beautiful. It's glorious. It's the reason you're who you are. It's the reason you've been given what you have. Do you remember all those incredible things? Oh, please don't forget them. Please *never* forget them. When you go off to whatever place is next for you in your life's journey, I'd love to think that the truths you've learned in this little Bible study book will go traveling with you, reminding you of your accepted, beloved, chosen, forgiven identity in Jesus.

That's *you*. It is *so* you.

But your ability to live in light of that identity will always require effort. Don't believe anybody who tells you otherwise. Remaining in neutral will always take you backward. The world will always seek to devalue every facet of who God has made you to be physically (your race, your gender, your unique gifting and abilities), as well as who you've now become by being reborn spiritually. If you don't actively fight against the current that is constantly pushing against you—renewing your mind in God's Word, surrounding yourself with the right influences, steering clear of activities and people who pull you away from the truth—you'll be swept up in the vicious waves and taken further downstream than you ever thought possible.

So as we come to the end of our time together—which my goodness, I hope you know how much I've enjoyed every moment we've been able to visit and talk with each other—I want to send you out with a charge and a promise. Life is going to be difficult. Life is difficult already. (I'm sure you've noticed.) Not sugarcoating that. But everything you need, God has promised to supply. Just you watch.

Let's finish with this final takeaway.

Whenever the Bible says we need to do something "above all else," we obviously need to be sure this verse gets placed on the top shelf. Top priority.

> Guard your heart above all else, for it is the source of life.
> *PROVERBS 4:23*

What does the verse above tell you to do "above all else"? Why?

Your heart needs to be *guarded*–because your heart will drive your decisions. The things you want to do will ultimately end up being the things you actually do. That's just the way it works. So we need our hearts to *want* to follow God, to obey His Word, to line up with our identity and who He's created and called us to be.

But naturally they don't. They don't want that. (I'm sure you've noticed that, too.) So what do we do? How do we get our hearts *wanting* God's will and His best intentions for us?

> **Look up Psalm 37:4. Before moving on, which of these four statements best summarizes the meaning of this verse?**
>
> **A. The things you want are not wrong; just start praying about them more.**
>
> **B. Growing in your love for God will align your desires with His desires.**
>
> **C. If you want something bad enough, God will eventually give it to you.**
>
> **D. God is happiest when you are happy.**

"Take delight in the LORD," Psalm 37:4 says–your Bible may say, "Delight yourself in the LORD"–"and he will give you your heart's desires." If this sounds like God is some kind of rich uncle, giving you whatever you want if you just ask for it nicely enough, you're reading it wrong. I hope you selected "B" from the choices above, because when you, as a woman of God, choose to honor and cooperate with the Holy Spirit's work in your life, He will begin to shift your desires. You'll see it. He actually gives you His desires and causes your wants to line up with His wants by infusing His own wants in you. This heart you've chosen to guard will now become a heart He's able to grow into a heart that will take you *by choice* where your identity knows it should go.

That's because when the Holy Spirit took up residence in your life, He came with a fruit basket. It was His housewarming gift to you. It's always been available to you. The only reason you may not have recognized it is because you haven't *guarded* your heart from invaders, both from without and within, that eat up everything before you're able to enjoy it.

But thanks be to God, the Holy Spirit is still there. And His fruit basket is still there, ever replenishing. And if you will determine with me–today–that you are really going to start cooperating with Him in your transformation, so the awesomeness of your identity can start translating into the abundance of your life with Him, you're about to witness a fruit explosion.

Allow me to demonstrate.

From Galatians 5:22-23, list the fruit that's sure to become evident in your life as you allow the Holy Spirit to change your desires. (Nine are listed.)

1.

2.

3.

4.

5.

6.

7.

8.

9.

Three things I'd like you to notice here:

1. Fruit is *visible*. You've never seen an invisible apple or an invisible pear. (I hope.) By virtue of its nature, fruit is a tangible item that can be seen, desired, picked, and handled.

2. Fruit is *identifiable*. It always reflects the nature of the tree it came from. You'll never see watermelons growing on a grapevine. Fruit carries the unique DNA of its source plant.

3. Fruit has a *purpose*. And its purpose is to be enjoyed by others, to give them nourishment. The only fruit that eats itself is a rotten one. Fruit is designed to share health with someone else.

Choose one of the fruit of God's Spirit you listed earlier. How can it be:

• **visible to you and others today?**

• **recognizable through your life today?**

- **beneficial to someone else today?**

Here's something unique about the fruit of the Spirit that ought to really excite you when you think about working with Him to align your identity with your lifestyle and mission.

Does Galatians 5:22 call these the "fruits of the Spirit" (plural) or the "fruit of the Spirit" (singular)?

"Fruit." Singular. Of these nine (and others) that are indicative of God's work inside you, there is actually just one "fruit" of the Spirit. The ones you listed are really flavors of the *one* fruit, the main fruit, which is simply a Spirit-controlled life. And so as you open up your heart to let Him "ooze" out from within you, all this fruit will start sprouting all at once. You won't need to worry if you can juggle them all. The one "fruit" will just take over your whole life, until you're running over with *all* kinds of evidence that God is at work in your life.

And because it comes from Him, it'll look like who you really are.

Since it comes from Him, it'll reflect the fullness of your inheritance.

The fruit that comes from Him will bless you and everyone around you.

So daughter, go into your world as a reflection of His grace and goodness. Live unapologetically and unashamedly as a follower of Jesus Christ, filled up with His Spirit, fashioned for His purpose and on mission for His Kingdom.

Today.

And everyday.

In Jesus name, Amen.

LEADER GUIDE

LEADER GUIDE TIPS

Pray diligently.

Ask God to prepare you to lead this study. Pray individually and specifically for the girls in your group. Make this a priority in your personal walk and preparation.

Prepare adequately.

Don't just wing this. Take time to preview each session so you have a good grasp of the content. Look over the group session and consider your girls. Feel free to delete or reword the questions provided, and add other questions that fit your group better.

Provide resources.

Each student will need a Bible study book. Try to have extras on hand for girls who join the group later in the study. Also suggest girls bring a Bible and journal to group each week.

Encourage freely.

Cheer for your girls and encourage them to participate in every part of the study.

Lead by example.

Make sure you complete all of the personal study. Be willing to share your story, what you're learning, and your questions as you discuss together.

Be aware.

If girls are hesitant to discuss their thoughts and questions in a larger group, consider dividing into smaller groups to provide a setting more conducive to conversation.

Follow up.

If a student mentions a prayer request or need, make sure to follow up. It may be a situation where you can get others in the group involved in helping out.

Evaluate often.

After each session and throughout the study, assess what needs to be changed to more effectively lead the study.

LEADER GUIDE

WEEK 1
UNIQUELY CREATED

FOR STARTERS: Kick off your group time together by getting to know your girls and helping them get to know each other. Our time together is going to demand honest sharing and vulnerability and that begins now! Consider breaking the ice with a game of two truths and a lie or another similar get-to-know-you game. Once your group is ready to start, you can jump straight into the Week 1 video.

PRESS PLAY: Begin your time together by watching the video. Discuss any important ideas or passages that jumped out at you and take some time to answer the questions together.

LET'S TALK: Our focus for this week will be on who we are. Make sure to spend time together figuring out who we are as daughters of the King. This means getting your girls to go so much deeper than tall or short, blonde or brunette. Discovering and locking down on who we really are is going to be the launching point for this entire study.

Spend as much time as you need in this first week letting girls consider their identity. Not based on their feelings or what they've been told by parents, teachers, coaches, friends, or bullies. But based on who they really are. Based on who God says they are.

CLOSING: Wrap up your group time together in prayer. Thank God for who He has created you to be and for the plans He has to use you in this time for His purposes. Follow up with your girls throughout the week to encourage them to stick with the days of personal study.

WEEK 2
STRUGGLES AND SOLUTIONS

FOR STARTERS: Today we are going to be talking about our biggest sins and struggles. This might be difficult for some, but it is going to be a very important part of finding our true identities. In preparation of fighting our sins, set up a thumb war bracket for your girls. Award a small prize to the undefeated Thumb War Champion!

PRESS PLAY: Before you begin the Week 2 video, spend a few minutes going over the personal study from Week 1. Answer any questions and share a few take-aways from the week. Continue with the video and take notes as you follow along.

LET'S TALK: As you work through the session together, spend some extra time identifying your girls' biggest struggles on page 38. Remind girls that your group is a safe place where they can be open and honest. Consider sharing some of your own struggles first to further encourage girls to share. Make sure to bring paper for them to write out their declarations. The girls may also need some help thinking of ways they can declare war against their struggles on page 39. Accountability partners are one strong way of forming battle lines against our sins and being intentional about the environments we find ourselves in.

CLOSING: As you close this week in prayer, remind your girls that you are ready and available to meet with them at any time. Welcome them to reach out to you if they are struggling with certain sins in their lives and don't know how to move forward. We were made for community.

WEEK 3
VITAL SIGNS

FOR STARTERS: Today we are going to discuss what it means to live as God's masterpiece. Find some molding clay or Play-Doh and hand out a designated amount to each girl. Set a timer for five minutes and direct girls use the clay to create their own piece of art. The only catch is that their creation has to have a specific function or purpose. When they finish, let each girl share her art with the group and talk about its purpose and what makes it special. Take a vote as a group on who has the best masterpiece!

PRESS PLAY: Before you begin the Week 3 video, spend a few minutes going over the personal study from Week 2. Answer any questions and share a few take-aways from the week. Continue with the video and take notes as you follow along.

LET'S TALK: This week we are going to focus on establishing a firm connection with Jesus. If we are not relying on Him and giving God our full praise and attention, then we will not be able to produce good fruit. Our discussion today has a short quiz. Encourage girls to take as much time as they need to complete the five questions honestly. There is no shame in wherever we may be in our relationship with God. Before moving on, be sure to identify any girls that are truly struggling and may need some extra encouragement during the week.

CLOSING: As you close in prayer, remind girls that God's promises are true. He is for us and wants us to be all-in for Him. He knows us and wants us to know Him, too.

WEEK 4
WHO YOU ARE

FOR STARTERS: Begin today by giving the girls a chance to give themselves a new name. Tell them that they can choose any name they want and have them share their new name with the group. Challenge them to refer to each other only by their new names for the rest of the group time. Today will focus on the fact that only God defines our identity, and no name, sin, stigma, or person can change that.

PRESS PLAY: Before you begin the Week 4 video, spend a few minutes going over the personal study from Week 3. Answer any questions and share a few take-aways from the week. Continue with the video and take notes as you follow along.

LET'S TALK: We've got a big assignment for this week. In groups of two or three, have your girls read through Ephesians 1–2 and point out every time it says who we are as believers. As the girls take turns reading the Scripture, encourage them to write down all of the "Who You Are" statements they find. Come back together as a group and compare your statements. Consider which statements are easiest to believe and which are more difficult as you challenge girls to live in the truth of these statements.

CLOSING: Close in prayer, specifically praying that girls will use this week to better understand who they are: chosen, loved, daughters of the King.

WEEK 5
WHAT YOU HAVE

FOR STARTERS: Today is going to highlight our spiritual inheritance as daughters of the King. Begin your time by creating an imaginary scenario with the girls. Tell them someone has left them an inheritance of a million dollars, and they can spend it however they would like. Ask the girls to share how they would spend their newfound fortune.

PRESS PLAY: Spend a few minutes going over the personal study from Week 4. Before you closed your time together last week, you identified the statements you thought were the most difficult to believe. Did that remain true for the whole week? Or were you able to grow in the confidence of your identity in Christ? Ask girls which of the "Who You Are" statements really stuck with them. Continue with the Week 5 video and take notes as you follow along.

LET'S TALK: This week is going to seem like a lot, but don't let your girls get discouraged. Last week, we listed everything we *are* according to Ephesians 1–2. In our time together today, we are going to look at that same passage of Scripture and start listing everything Ephesians 1–2 says we *have*. There are a few examples included to get you going on page 110. Encourage girls to use a journal or an extra piece of paper to write down all the blessings they discover in Ephesians.

CLOSING: As you close in prayer, praise God for all the blessings we have received as His children. Encourage girls to list something they are thankful for each night as they complete their personal study days, and don't forget to start each day with the assigned verses on page 110.

WEEK 6
WALK THIS WAY

FOR STARTERS: Today we will be discussing the idea of walking in the spiritual identity that God has given each of us. As you begin, ask girls to talk about a time when they learned something new. Whether it was when they learned how to drive or when they learned how to swim, encourage each girl to share a personal story about her learning experience and what it took for her to succeed.

PRESS PLAY: This last week of personal study was a big one. We covered a lot, so spend as much time as you need here. Give each girl a chance to share her favorite "I have" statements and share a few from your own list. Continue with the video for Week 6 and take notes as you follow along.

LET'S TALK: Looking like Jesus means following in His footsteps and walking the way He walked. The only way we will become more and more like Him is with intentional steps. Before jumping into the chart on page 134, read through the description that follows and complete one together using your own example of walking.

CLOSING: Close in prayer and remind girls that with every step toward Christ, they are walking in their new identity as a child of God. Consistent practice and concentration on their steps today will become confident strides in their faith for the days to come.

WEEK 7
IN CHRIST, ON PURPOSE

FOR STARTERS: Each of us has been given a specific mission by God to live out in our lives. Before you jump into today's lesson, play a short game of charades with your girls. Give each girl a piece of paper with something she will have to act out to the entire group. Time each girl to see how long it takes the group to guess what she's doing. Whoever portrays their action the fastest is the winner!

PRESS PLAY: This last week of personal study was filled with practical steps. Invite girls to share any ideas they had for helping themselves and their friends to walk better. Then jump into the video for Week 7.

LET'S TALK: You will need some colored pencils for today's lesson. We will be creating a picture of how walking in obedience leads to growing in our relationship with the Holy Spirit. Those seeds we have been planting since the first week are going to continue to grow inside of us as we are transformed from the inside out.

This week's discussion starts out with a topic that may be difficult for some girls. You know your group better than anyone else, so address the topic in the best way for your girls.

CLOSING: As you wrap up, pray for girls to have the endurance to live on mission every day. This is our last week of personal study, so make sure to encourage girls to finish strong and be ready for the celebration of our final week together defining our identity.

WEEK 8
GUARDING YOUR IDENTITY

FOR STARTERS: It's our final time together, and I pray that you walk away from this last week knowing with confidence who you are in Christ. Today we will talk about the importance of the fruit of the Spirit as you walk in faith. To help girls remember the fruit of the Spirit listed in Galatians 5:22-23, play a game of Memes of the Spirit. Challenge each girl to find a meme or gif that best exemplifies one fruit of the Spirit. Share your selections and vote on the best one. Since it's the last day, consider meeting for dinner or having ice cream sundaes to celebrate.

PRESS PLAY: Go over any questions from Week 7, and list a few ways you have personally seen your life change over the last eight weeks. Encourage the girls to share how this study has impacted their walk with God, and what they hope will stick with them the most. Spend a few minutes reviewing all the places we have been before playing the Week 8 video.

LET'S TALK: Now that we know we have the Holy Spirit inside us, we have to guard our hearts against the enemy. As we fend off attacks, we will grow in the fruit of the Spirit that is in us already and ready to flourish. Discuss examples of what the fruit of the Spirit should look like displayed in real life.

CLOSING: Close your final day with prayer over all of your girls for strength and peace to walk confidently in their identity. Consider a popcorn prayer allowing girls to pray for one another and for their own next steps as they live out their true, God-given identities.

ENDNOTES

WEEK 1

1. "New Strings," *Nashville*, directed by Timothy Busfield (Country Music Television, Inc.), January 4 2018.
2. "identity," *Oxford English Dictionary*. Oxford University Press, 2019. https://en.oxforddictionaries.com/definition/identity.
3. One place you can do this is online at *blueletterbible.org*.
4. J. B. Polhill, "Acts," *NAC* (Nashville: Broadman & Holman, 1992), 372.
5. Hendriksen and Kistemaker, *Exposition of Paul's Epistle to the Romans.* (Grand Rapids: Baker, 1953), 72.

WEEK 2

1. A. Hay, "Original Sin," from *The Lexham Bible Dictionary* (Bellingham, WA: Lexham Press, 2016).
2. Rick Warren, *The Purpose Driven Life* (Grand Rapids, MI: Zondervan, 2002), pg. 265.
3. Tony Evans, *Theology You Can Count On* (Chicago: Moody Publishers, 2008), 759.

WEEK 3

1. "*meno*," Blue Letter Bible, Strong's 3306. Available online at *blueletterbible.org*.
2. Dr. Daniel L. Akin, *Christ-Centered Exposition Commentary: Exalting Jesus in 1, 2, & 3 John* (Nashville, TN: B&H Publishing Group, 2014), 115.

WEEK 4

1. *Overcomer*, directed by Alex Kendrick (Culver City, CA: Sony Pictures, 2019), Film.
2. "*poiema*," Blue Letter Bible, Strong's 4161. Available online at *blueletterbible.org*.
3. Tony Merida, *Christ-Centered Exposition: Exalting Jesus in Ephesians* (Nashville, TN: 2014) 52.

WEEK 5

1. "*charis*," Blue Letter Bible, Strong's 5485. Available online at *blueletterbible.org*.
2. William Hendrikson, *New Testament Commentary: Exposition of Ephesians* (Grand Rapids, MI: Baker Book House, 1968), 71.
3. P.T. O'Brien, *The Letter to the Ephesians* (Grand Rapids, MI: Eerdmans, 1999), 115.

WEEK 6

1. Philip Jenkins, *The Next Christendom* (New York: Oxford University Press, 2011).
2. Aaron Earls, "Most Teenagers Drop Out of Church as Young Adults," *LifeWay Research*, January 15, 2019, https://lifewayresearch.com/2019/01/15/most-teenagers-drop-out-of-church-as-young-adults/.

WEEK 7

1. Scholars hold varying opinions on whether the spirit and soul are two separate parts of our makeup or are actually interchangeable terms. Either way, the lessons of this exercise hold true. I'm leaning on 1 Thessalonians 5:23, where Paul uses all three terms: "spirit, soul, and body."

MY IDENTITY AND INHERITANCE IN CHRIST

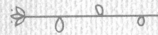

The benefits and blessings bestowed upon us as redeemed children of God are more numerous than we can count. Here is a sampling taken directly from Scripture.

Read it. Rehearse it. Believe it.

- I am a child of God (John 1:12).
- I have peace with God (Rom. 5:1).
- The Holy Spirit lives in me (1 Cor. 3:16).
- I have access to God's wisdom (Jas. 1:5).
- I am helped by God (Heb. 4:16).
- I am reconciled to God (Rom. 5:11).
- I am not condemned by God (Rom. 8:1).
- I am justified (Rom. 5:1).
- I have Christ's righteousness (Rom. 5:19; 2 Cor. 5:21).
- I am Christ's ambassador (2 Cor. 5:20).
- I am completely forgiven (Col. 1:14).
- I am tenderly loved by God (Jer. 31:3).
- I am the sweet fragrance of Christ to God (2 Cor. 2:15).
- I am a temple in which God dwells (1 Cor. 3:16).
- I am blameless and beyond reproach (Col. 1:22).
- I am the salt of the earth (Matt. 5:13).
- I am the light of the world (Matt. 5:14).
- I am a branch on Christ's vine (John 15:1,5).
- I am Christ's friend (John 15:5).
- I am chosen by Christ to bear fruit (John 15:6).
- I am a joint heir with Christ, sharing his inheritance with him (Rom. 8:17).
- I am united to the Lord, one spirit with him (1 Cor. 6:17).
- I am a member of Christ's body (1 Cor. 12:27).
- I am a saint (Eph. 1:1).
- I am hidden with Christ in God (Col. 3:3).
- I am chosen by God, holy and dearly loved (Col. 3:12).
- I am a child of the light (1 Thess. 5:5).
- I am holy, and I share in God's heavenly calling (Heb. 3:1).
- I am sanctified (Heb. 2:11).
- I am one of God's living stones, being built up in Christ as a spiritual house (1 Pet. 2:5).
- I am a member of a chosen race, a royal priesthood, a holy nation, a people for God's own possession and created to sing his praises (1 Pet. 2:9-10).
- I am firmly rooted and built up in Christ (Col. 2:7).
- I am born of God, and the evil one cannot touch me (1 John 5:18).
- I have the mind of Christ (1 Cor. 2:16).
- I may approach God with boldness, freedom, and confidence (Eph. 3:12).
- I have been rescued from Satan's domain and transferred into the kingdom of Christ (Col. 1:13).
- I have been made complete in Christ (Col. 2:10).
- I have been given a spirit of power, love, and self-discipline (2 Tim. 1:7).
- I have been given great and precious promises by God (2 Pet. 1:4).
- My needs are met by God (Phil. 4:19).
- I am a prince (princess) in God's kingdom (John 1:12; 1 Tim. 6:15).
- I have been bought with a price, and I belong to God (1 Cor. 6:19,20).
- I have been adopted as God's child (Eph. 1:5).
- I have direct access to God through the Holy Spirit (Eph. 2:18).
- I am assured that all things are working together for good (Rom. 8:28).
- I am free from any condemning charges against me (Rom. 8:31).
- I cannot be separated from the love of God (Rom. 8:35).
- I have been established, anointed, and sealed by God (2 Cor. 1:21,22).
- I am confident that the good work that God has begun in me will be perfected (Phil. 1:6).
- I am a citizen of heaven (Phil. 3:20).
- I am a personal witness of Christ's (Acts 1:8).
- I am God's coworker (2 Cor. 6:1; 1 Cor. 3:9).
- I am seated with Christ in the heavenly realm (Eph. 2:6).
- I am God's workmanship (Eph. 2:10).
- I can do all things through Christ, who gives me the strength I need (Phil. 4:13).